Flyover People

Life on the Ground in a Rectangular State

(meaning the title - you each get one)
I'm sending this book to my expatriate sister & brother to remind them and because their older sis is on p. 93! Happy birthday - you've almost caught up to me.
Love,
11/13ish/10

Cheryl Unruh

2010

Quincy Press

Flyover People: Life on the Ground in a Rectangular State

Quincy Press
Box 1215
Emporia, KS 66801
www.quincypress.com

Used with permission: Annie Wilson's lyrics in "Kaw Trail," "Clean Curve of Hill Against Sky" and "The Moon Can Take Me Home," from the CD *Clean Curve of Hill Against Sky* by the Tallgrass Express String Band.

All photographs on the cover and inside the book are by Dave Leiker, with the exception of the photo on Page 115, which was taken by Anita Byers.

Book design and editing by Leon Unruh.

ISBN 978-0-615-38534-1

Library of Congress Control Number: 2010910709

Printed by Mennonite Press, Inc., in Newton, Kansas, USA.

Flyover People

Life on the Ground in a Rectangular State

For Dave, who makes the journey fun.

And for my mom, my dad and my brother.

CONTENTS

Seasons

Nature

Looking Back

Childhood

ACKNOWLEDGMENTS

I owe so much to Dave. His presence sustains me.

I send an ocean of gratitude to my brother and editor, Leon Unruh. There's no one I trust with my words more than Leon. His involvement in the project turned this book into a reality.

A hug of appreciation goes to my mother for her unconditional support and encouragement since Day One. I am grateful to my father, who showed by example that Kansas is worth exploring. Thanks go to my Aunt Norma, a magical source of creative energy, and to my late Uncle Jay for being proud of me even though I wrote about flat land.

Much appreciation goes to the staff (past and present) at *The Emporia Gazette,* which has provided the opportunity for me to share my words with readers. I extend a gracious thank you to the fine folks at Kansas Public Radio in Lawrence for allowing me to be one of their commentators, and to the staff at KTWU, public television in Topeka, for also giving me a bit of airtime.

To longtime friends and Flyover friends, thank you for being my cheer squad. The buoyancy you offer daily keeps me afloat and keeps me spilling words onto the page. Special thanks to: Tracy, Roger, Janet, Ele, April, Simon, Onnalee, Jay, Amy, Marilyn, Ray, Peg, Kris, Eve and Wendy.

I offer a humble bow to my faithful readers. You rock my world.

INTRODUCTION

During the summer of 2002, I began pestering the editors at *The Emporia Gazette,* asking for a chance to write a freelance column for the paper. On January 28, 2003, the day before Kansas Day, my first "Flyover People" column was published. That was a very happy day.

The columns in this collection have appeared in *The Gazette,* although most have been altered in some way for this book. It has been an honor to contribute to William Allen White's Pulitzer Prize–winning newspaper, which is still family-owned.

As a writer, I can't think of a subject I'd rather cover each week than the great state of Kansas—its small towns, the weather, the people, the landscape. I love this place.

Now, of course, I'd love Kansas more if it had less winter, but things are the way they are and this is home.

My late Uncle Jay once suggested that I move to Arkansas and write there. He said, "Heck, anyone who can find inspiration in Kansas could go great guns down here."

Jay could never understand my nonnegotiable love for the prairie, its level horizon, our changing skies.

But you, my fellow plainsmen, I know good and well that you understand.

Pure Kansas

January 2003

ON BEING A KANSAN

I've leaned into the Kansas wind for 43 years. My life began 150 miles west of here, in Pawnee Rock, a dirt-street town with familiar faces, loose dogs and few opportunities. At 18, I fled.

But, as you may have noticed, I didn't get far. Yes, Toto, I'm still in Kansas, along with 2.7 million other people.

Why do we stay? What keeps us in Kansas? Is it family ties? Do we really love the place, or are we just too stupid to leave?

In 2001, Jay Price, a history professor at Wichita State University, came to Emporia to give a Kansas Humanities presentation titled "Reading Roadside Kansas." I spoke with him afterward and we've continued an endless discussion of regional identity by e-mail. (Jay, incidentally, had only lived in Kansas for two years.)

One of the first questions he sent me was, "What's your take on what it means to be a Kansan?"

What does it mean to be a Kansan? That was too big of a question. I dodged it by responding, "To consider myself a Kansan, I am defining myself with lines drawn by someone else."

True, perhaps. And those invisible state lines do make us different somehow from Okies. But being a Kansan is more than residing within its borders. How can you take a lifetime of living here and condense it into a paragraph? And when you explain your appreciation of Kansas to a non-Kansan, it all sounds so silly. ("Yes we like the nothingness. No, really, we do.")

I don't know what it means to be a Kansan, but I can describe the days. Sometimes we wouldn't have clouds if not for the jet trails that mark the sky. Our eyes travel miles ahead in western Kansas, catching sight of the grain elevator in the next town, the only vertical distraction. In the Flint Hills, the grass and sky may look plain and simple, but once you step onto the land and take a deep breath, it can change you forever.

Not all Kansans have had the same experiences, but quite a few have tasted the stringiness of cottonwood fluff. Some know the soft dust on harvested wheat and the quicksand feeling of stepping into a pile of grain loaded in a farm truck. Many of us hear trains whistle through town, calling to the night like coyotes.

Memories and experiences become part of who we are. Kansas seeps into our cells, reconfigures our DNA, claims us as its own. If we leave, it follows. William Inge, the playwright from Independence, said, "It wasn't until I got to New York that I became a Kansan."

What does it mean to be a Kansan? I'm not sure. Maybe I'll never figure it out. But I do know that if we look beyond the jets that stripe our sky, we learn all the shades of blue. If we gaze deep enough into that blue, we understand infinity.

That's why we stay.

March 2003

KANSAS GOES ALL THE WAY UP

Occasionally I meet in Strong City with three Chase County women to discuss writing and such things. So one winter's evening, I emerged from hibernation and drove westbound on U.S. Highway 50.

By the time I hit the open road, the early-to-bed sun had just dropped below the southwestern edge of earth. Now showing on the wide-screen drive-in theatre was a rose-colored sunset.

A stream of pastel clouds lined the horizon. As I stared into the evolving color, glints of light became apparent.

Jets, eight of them, glimmered in the sunset like UFOs, silver platters against petal-pink sky. Caught in the vision of the disappearing sun, each spark was aimed at random, headed for who knows where.

Even when jets don't appear to be UFOs, I am captivated by the planes and the thin, crisp vapor trails that chase them. Miles above us, people travel toward adventure, leaving a path of bread crumbs in the air behind them.

Encased in aerodynamic sheets of metal, a hundred or more people scoot across the sky, each person with her own story, each one focused on his destination. As the planes draw a steady white line, I wonder which passenger flies toward a beach in the Caribbean, which one anticipates a lover's reunion in Miami and which traveler hopes he'll just be able to find his car in the airport parking lot.

I imagined those eight planes, glowing in the western sky, to be full of restless magazine readers, sipping 7Up, glancing out thick windows down to the Flint Hills. I wondered what they'd see, peering down to the prairie at dusk. Does the cluster of street lights from Strong City show up at 30,000 feet? Will their eyes catch headlights on a long stretch of highway?

I call this column "Flyover People" because of my fascination with the sky, the sunsets, the clouds, as well as the planes and travelers that inhabit the air. The phrase flyover people is intended as a disparaging term by the jet-setters from the East and West coasts who feel a little superior to those of us living in the slower-paced rural Midwest. They get impatient while crossing our wide expanse of farmland.

In *Great Plains,* Ian Frazier writes, "America is like a wave of higher and higher frequency toward each end, and lowest frequency in the middle." He's right, but it's OK to be the eye in the center of the storm.

Personally, I don't mind being considered inconsequential to those jet-setters. I like being flown over. It makes me feel connected with the animated sky. And around here, the sky is not just above, but in front, behind and beside us.

In the 1970s, Vern Miller, our somewhat hyperactive Kansas attorney general, wanted to enforce Kansas' liquor laws in the airplanes flying over the state. He is said to have proclaimed, "Kansas goes all the way up, and Kansas goes all the way down."

Our endless sky does belong to us. It is ever-present, a player in our daily lives.

For a few days immediately following Sept. 11, 2001, air traffic was grounded. Without contrails streaking the sky, this was a lonely place. Our constant companions had disappeared. The gypsies in the sky were gone: the business travelers, the vacationers, the flight attendants and their beverage carts.

Airplanes garner a moment's more attention since we first heard those words, ". . . and a field in Pennsylvania." Now when we spy a shiny piece of metal in the air, a needle pulling thread, we pause, parent-like, to follow that plane to its vanishing point, until it disappears into thin air.

Jets sprint through the atmosphere, leaving momentary footprints on the sky. Inside the pressurized cabin, a passenger, headed for who knows where, leans her brow against the cool window to catch a glimpse of life on the ground in a rectangular state.

And we are down here, looking up.

January 2004

ONE HUNDRED FORTY-THREE

By now, you've probably grown tired of everyone asking, "Are you ready for Kansas Day?"

You've finished the Kansas Day baking and decorated your house with wheat bouquets. A sunflower wreath hangs on your front door.

OK, I'm just kidding. My guess is that you won't be slicing a meadowlark-shaped birthday cake this week.

Gov. Sebelius and her gang in Topeka will probably celebrate the day with cake and punch. And I'll bet that in grade schools across the state, there will be a few classroom parties.

The rest of us have forgotten to celebrate Kansas Day.

I don't know who's in charge of slogans, but "We're No. 34!" isn't exactly what we had in mind.

Maybe we need a state hero to rev things up, a spokesperson, or perhaps something like GEICO's gecko. A spokes-lizard. The barred tiger salamander is the state amphibian, but alas, salamanders have no voice.

We have a state animal, the American bison, and a state insect, the honeybee. The ornate box turtle serves as our official state reptile.

Sadly, we have no mascot. Neither the Jayhawk nor the Wildcat is representative of the entire state. There's Dorothy, of course, but she's kind of a lost soul, tossed about by the wind.

And Kansas has no official state colors so we wouldn't even know what color of streamers to hang from the ceilings. (I vote for wheat gold and sky blue.)

I suppose part of the Kansas Day apathy is that it falls at the end of January, when all the fun has gone out of winter. These are usually the coldest days of the season and people are still recovering from the recent go-round of actual holidays.

The winter doldrums are here. There's the Super Bowl but then it's a long stretch before that first strikeout of April. That leaves golf and basketball to fall asleep to on Sunday afternoon couches or, if you can find it, a bowling tournament.

Regardless of the lack of statewide enthusiasm, ever since we joined the union in 1861, Kansas Day comes around each Jan. 29.

Last January, I discovered a University of Kansas Alumni Web page announcing a celebration in San Diego. These Californians planned a beach party in honor of Kansas Day. A beach party! Why didn't we think of that?

Kansas Day could be fun: parades and dances, sunflower-seed spitting contests. Lions Clubs in each town could put on buffalo burger feeds.

We could play silly Kansas games. Twister, for example.

When my brother visited last fall, we played the old Kansas game—counties and county seats. Even though he's lived outside the state for most of the past 20-some years, Leon remembers his Kansas geography.

Our sixth-grade teacher, Elva Jean Latas, made each class memorize the 105 counties and their county seats. We learned 21 counties at a time. Eventually, we had a blank sheet of paper and were expected to pull the whole darned state out of our heads.

This was the stuff that my brother and I lived for. So when Leon was here, we stayed up late and named the counties.

"Sherman, Goodland," I said.

"Jewell, Mankato," Leon countered.

"Good one. Bourbon, Fort Scott. I've always remembered that one as Bourbon, Fort Scotch," I said.

After naming all that we could, we got out the map. We'd overlooked two of them: Brown, Hiawatha, and Kearny, Lakin.

Maybe it's not too late to plan a Kansas Day party. Inflate the balloons, hang the streamers, study the counties and county seats.

How about a costume party? Guests could dress up as Nurse Clara Barton (Barton, Great Bend) or newspaper editor Horace Greeley (Greeley, Tribune) or Wabaunsee, a Potawatomi chief (Wabaunsee, Alma.)

And don't forget to buy 143 candles. Happy Kansas Day.

June 2006

GROUNDED

Driving through Greenwood County on Memorial Day, Dave and I stop in at Reece.

Reece is an unincorporated town located about nine miles west of Eureka and just south of U.S. Highway 54. The road through the community has five sharp curves, a departure from the traditional straight streets of Kansas towns.

"It's a little Ozarky, isn't it?" Dave asks, as we wind through the woodsy village.

At the south end of town we discover a junk yard that was not open for business and probably hadn't been for 20 years. The place is overgrown with thickets and trees. Behind the foliage and car parts, a wooden house and numerous outbuildings are coming apart board by board. From the road, I admire the colors and shapes: a blue bus, a yellow one, a green Chevy truck cab and an assortment of tires, tools and metal.

I'm my father's daughter—I enjoy looking at old machinery and used-up school buses that were abandoned three or four decades ago.

To me, a junk yard is similar to, but maybe better than, a museum. Nothing is polished or clean or in perfect condition. A person gets a more intimate feel for the life and times of days gone by because you see the tools and vehicles outdoors, in their natural habitat.

There sits a GMC school bus, its yellow paint losing the battle to rust. I can imagine children riding that bus and bouncing on the seats—until the kids glance at the driver's overhead mirror and catch his disapproving eye.

The round fenders of the green Chevy truck cab bring to mind my dad's old pickup, the one with the manual choke, a two-piece windshield, and a rotting-out wooden bed that a kid could watch the ground through when she rode in the back of the truck.

In rural Kansas, we never get too far, in time or distance, from where we started. We are connected to this place and the past, in every phase of its delightful rustiness.

Earlier that morning before visiting Reece, Dave and I had pulled off Kansas Highway 99 and walked around downtown Hamilton, taking photographs. In cities, which have so many buildings in a row, the downtown becomes a blur. But in a tiny town, each storefront jumps out, eager to tell you its past. Like layers of wallpaper, each tenant leaves a layer of history on a building.

A top-heavy, lopsided elm stands against Holmes Sundries. If I were from Hamilton, that is a picture I would remember all my life. The tree is as much a part of the town as any building there.

South of Hamilton we stop at the Utopia Community Church, a remnant of the town named Utopia. The two-story farmhouse-turned-church-turned-abandoned-building is being lost to time and weather. In the yard, knee-high grass bows in the light breeze. Here, the quietness of the country settles like dust. The gravel road stretches on to the west, disappearing over a rise.

It occurs to me how glad I am to live in Kansas, to stand on the land and be surrounded by vast space. To know the sky so well. To see green pastures undulate for miles until distance swallows form.

I think many of us feel an innate connection to the earth, whether we're out in the country or in a town like Hamilton. We never lose this sense of being grounded, of knowing who we are and why we're here, of being nurtured by the soil and the grass and the stars.

Buses and buildings decay. But we understand the timelessness of the prairie. We will always be a part of the land. We will always be a part of that which does not change.

November 2006

HOME ON THE RANGE

I slammed on the brakes.

A sign along U.S. Highway 36 near the tiny town of Athol pointed the way to the "Home on the Range" cabin.

"Hang on. We have to see that!" I told Dave as I made the sharp right turn.

When her book, *The Kansas Guidebook for Explorers,* was published last year, Marci Penner told me that the "Home on the Range" cabin was the one place, if she had to name one, that every Kansan should visit.

For some reason, I had pictured this cabin as being near the Colorado border, so I hadn't penciled it in on this trip. But what a nice surprise—and it was only nine miles away: eight north and one west.

The last mile was a narrow road that took us past milo fields rich with autumn colors. Where the road curved, we saw a family of turkeys slip through a barbed-wire fence. The small log cabin is on private property. Luckily, the landowners are willing to share this treasure, as was the black and white dog who rushed to greet us.

According to a brochure available inside the cabin, Dr. Brewster Higley was born in Ohio, received his medical degree in Indiana and eventually homesteaded here in Smith County, Kansas, in 1871. That brochure suggests that Higley wrote most of the verses of a poem he called "My Western Home" during the autumn of 1872. He then placed the manuscript inside a book. The next spring, a guest found the poem in the book and reportedly proclaimed, "Why Doc, that's plum good!"

Higley showed the poem to Daniel E. Kelley, a local composer, who came up with a tune. "My Western Home" was introduced at a community dance in April of 1873.

The song was passed around and altered and the names of the songwriters became lost.

President-elect Franklin D. Roosevelt announced his fondness for the tune in 1932 and soon it became a hit on the radio.

In 1934, an Arizona couple, who claimed to have written the song as "My Arizona Home," sued broadcasting and publishing companies for copyright infringement. During the legal scuffle, documentation found in the *Kirwin Chief* newspaper indicated that Dr. Higley had written the words more than 30 years before the Arizona couple's copyright had been registered.

"Home on the Range" was adopted by the Kansas Legislature as our official state song in 1947.

Dave and I visited Higley's cabin on a quiet October day. Grass and trees were still mostly green on the banks of Beaver Creek. From the cabin, Dr. Higley could probably hear the stream running at night. On the open land, he could gaze upon restless clouds, watch thunderstorms move in and see the stars beaming their light down to the Kansas prairie. He wrote:

How often at night when the heavens were bright
With the light of the twinkling stars
Have I stood here amazed and asked as I gazed
If their glory exceeds that of ours.

Wandering around the property, under the shelter of the trees along Beaver Creek, the thought that entered my mind was how could he live here and *not* write "Home on the Range"?

Butterflies linger on this grassy bank, and the warm autumn sun glows through the locust leaves. Words would flow like a stream here and a person could easily pen his love for the land, for the unclouded sky, for the caress of a soft wind.

The present-day lyrics are a bit different, but Higley wrote:

The air is so pure and the breeze is so fine
The zephyr so balmy and light
That I would not exchange my home here to range
Forever in azure so bright.

March 2004

FAR FROM THE MADDING CROWD

Generally speaking, it's a good thing to have other people around.

But in moderation, please.

Maybe Wyandotte County residents don't mind sharing a square mile with 1,042 other people, but that seems a little crowded to me.

And because I was already clicking around on the 2000 U.S. Census Web pages, I checked out New York County, N.Y., i.e., Manhattan. Stand back—New York County has 67,000 people to the square mile. Ouch. That is a tall stack of human beings.

But as Roger von Oech said, "Skyscrapers weren't built by people with a lot of land. . . ."

One of the best things about rural Kansas is that we have an abundance of land and not so many buildings. We have enough space to be ourselves.

Lyon County has an average of 42.2 people per square mile. As a state, Kansas averages 32.9. Area counties vary in population density: Greenwood 6.7, Coffey 14.1, Osage 23.8, Wabaunsee 8.6, Morris 8.8 and Chase 3.9.

The roominess expands in western Kansas. Wallace County, on the Colorado border, averages 1.9 persons to the square mile. Out there you can holler and shout if you want and no one will hear.

Kansas City is a different story. Dave and I were there not long ago and the parking lots in Overland Park were packed with vehicles. Every street was full of cars idling at stoplights. Six lanes. Eight lanes. Turn lanes. Cars, cars, everywhere.

The American Highway Users Alliance recently released a study of traffic congestion. A bottleneck is defined as a location that causes 700,000 annual hours of delay.

Kansas City isn't the biggest or busiest metropolitan area; it has only one bottleneck. Phoenix, Chicago, Detroit and Miami are full of them.

The trouble spot in Kansas City, Missouri, is the junction of Interstates 70 and 435. It carries 112,000 vehicles a day and is ranked 200th on the list of 233 bottlenecks.

Meanwhile, in Emporia, traffic flows well. Most of the time we get through an intersection on the first green light.

Perhaps we wait 30 seconds longer than we think we should have to on Graphic Arts Road before and after school, but let's count our blessings: We don't have 112,000 cars a day clogging our intersections and polluting our air.

A few of the bottlenecks do have some good nicknames. In Atlanta, they have Spaghetti Junction. Denver has The Mousetrap and Milwaukee, The Zoo. Orange County, California, has an interstate junction called Orange Crush. It carries 308,000 vehicles a day. The best-named bottleneck no longer exists. The Hillside Strangler in Chicago was a traffic tie-up five years ago, but reconstruction has loosened the noose.

The number of bottlenecks has jumped more than 40 percent over the past five years, from 167 choke points in 1999 to 233 this year.

Traffic on the city freeways moves either very slow or very fast. On that trip to Kansas City, Dave and I took I-35 through the peaceful countryside. As we approached the metro area, more and more speeding cars passed us.

"It's funny, but the closer you get to the city, the faster traffic goes," Dave said. "It's like when you're a kid on a merry-go-round and you're going fast and then everyone pulls in and the merry-go-round goes even faster."

The Good Sense Rule of one car length between vehicles for every 10 mph of speed does not seem to be applied in the city (or in NASCAR races, if you've noticed).

Still, everyone needs a buffer zone.

Although he was writing about marriage, Kahlil Gibran provides good advice for us all: "But let there be spaces in your togetherness, and let the winds of the heavens dance between you."

February 2008

PER ASPERA

After reports of Tyson's job cuts, I woke the next morning recalling the words of a new friend, a journalist from Denmark.

"There is a lot of pride and stamina among people in Kansas," Jonas Langvad Nilsson had said.

On his visit to our state last June, Nilsson saw Kansans for what we are—resilient and tough.

Some of our physical stamina surely comes from enduring the ever-present wind, which can be exhausting, yet we handle it. But much of our toughness comes from the hardships we encounter and overcome. Every Kansan can recite the state motto: Ad astra per aspera—to the stars through difficulties.

Difficulties surround us right now. Losing 1,500 jobs—suddenly and unexpectedly—is an agonizing blow to Emporia's Tyson workers and to the entire region.

Kansans are a plucky bunch and always have been. Those who have lived on this prairie have survived many trials.

Let's consider the early ones who led the way. Five and six generations ago, our forefathers settled the empty prairie, made Kansas their home.

In the early and mid-1800s, pioneers and Native Americans did not always greet each other with open arms. There were ferocious battles. People died. And then there was a battle with insects, the grasshopper plague of 1874, during which grasshoppers consumed pretty much every green thing.

It takes something more catastrophic than a billion insects, however, to dissuade a Kansan from staying put. Go ahead, grasshoppers, eat all our food, but we're here for the long haul.

Then there's the extreme weather. Some Kansans who homesteaded this state outlasted ice storms and blizzards while living in sod houses. And in the miserable heat and humidity, they plowed fields with their horses.

Many early Kansans traveled, worked and slept on the prairie during tremendous thunderstorms. (Lightning rods are us.) And just imagine the surprise when a settler saw his first tornado.

Here in the Flint Hills, our ancestors took on the backbreaking task of removing limestone chunks from fields in order to claim the land for crops.

When the railroads were built, sometimes the tracks bypassed small towns. A railroad connection was vital to a town's survival. So, what did the people in Cuba, Burdett, Beeler and Rochester do? Residents picked up their towns and moved them to the tracks. They did what they could to keep their communities alive.

Kansans faced cholera and the 1918 influenza epidemic. Then there were days in the 1930s when they inhaled more than the recommended daily allowance of dust. And somehow, for some reason, quite of few of the settlers stayed in Kansas; they built homes and communities.

Emporians experienced tornadoes in 1974 and 1990. Both times, we assessed the damage and we rebuilt.

And today, certainly, tough times are ahead for Emporia's displaced workers. They will be making countless decisions—where to go, what to do, how to sell their homes in a saturated market. Hopefully, in the long run, they will find good jobs and prosper wherever they land.

Tyson's decision will cause a variety of economic struggles for this area. This is a time for us to stand together, to support local businesses so money, sales tax receipts and jobs stay in town. And it's to our advantage to remain hopeful and positive.

As workers and as a community, we've been knocked down. Rising, we wipe the dust from our knees, assess the damage, and rebuild. We will move ourselves and our town to the railroad tracks, so to speak.

In working together, this may become our finest hour.

Life is full of difficulties, but we Kansans have always found our way to the stars.

April 2003

AH, KANSAS

Perched above Domino's Pizza, a billboard promotes Emporia. It also mentions National Tourism Week coming up in mid-May.

Prepare for the onslaught of vacationers. Or not.

As much as the state's Travel and Tourism Department would like it, people don't aim for Kansas. They stumble in, most likely on the way to their actual vacation destination. Kansas just happens to be in the way.

Several years ago, a rather odd state promotional slogan was "Drive through Kansas and you'll miss it," which seems to be entirely the point for many passers-through. But we encourage those drive-through tourists to linger longer, to spend a night in one of our motels, to eat chicken-fried steaks in one of our restaurants.

We're not a destination state and we know it. People seldom drop in unless they have relatives and come for that "We're not having a real vacation, we're visiting family" vacation. Few stop by for scenery or adventure. Nothing here but dirt, grass and sky as far as the eye can see, which actually is quite a few miles.

Travelers often miss the subtlety of the prairie. They'll never know how even green grass in the Flint Hills crunches like Corn Flakes. Only by hanging around will they discover that no two sunsets are alike and that the awkward angle of the October sun can make one feel out of sorts and never quite right again until March.

Stepping into the vastness and vacantness, one discovers a claustrophobia-free land. Kansas bares itself to the sky like a nude sunbather, open and honest. And only tiny secrets are hidden along the river banks, where trees gather like people at church dinners.

I know we're supposed to want tourists. Our state and local economies need them more than ever. But it's nice, too, to live in a place that's not crazy with traffic, where billboards are less frantic than one in Colorado: "Scream till Daddy stops."

Kansas is the place we retreat to after the crowds of the Grand Canyon, after the T-shirt shops of Estes Park. This is peace. This is home.

Our state may not seem like much of a draw. There are droughts, blizzards, dust storms, hail and tornadoes, sometimes all on the same day. We have chiggers, mosquitoes and wind.

Kansas illustrates an Amish geography: plain and modest. Nothing showy or ostentatious. It takes a patient person to savor the quiet landscape, to revel as clouds pull the day along.

And our sunsets are as vital as breath. The glowing sphere lights fire to the clouds and infuses the air with an itchy smell of grass. Night after night, I've watched our star stage its flashy farewell as trees become silhouettes. All color is pulled from the world as it chases the sun.

My name is on the deed to one tiny plot of land, but the entire state belongs to me: each meadowlark's song, a bull snake disappearing into the underworld, the bone-thin coyote slipping through the timber.

Essayist Rudolfo Anaya wrote, "The tourist cannot love the place as much as the native. We learn to love the land that nurtures us."

There is a connection to the land that can be felt here, a comfort in being where ground meets sky, that line of horizon that forever defines us as earth people. Welcome home, travelers.

Welcome home.

November 2006

THE BEACON

The green dome can be seen from afar.

A lighthouse for the prairie, the Kansas Capitol stands proud and tall on this land without a seashore. And at the top of the dome is Ad Astra, a Kansa warrior who points the way, guiding us through life's difficult stars.

Dave and I were in Topeka a few weeks ago and we drove past the Statehouse. I noticed the Abe Lincoln statue on the south lawn and stopped to take a photograph.

Some of the ground surrounding the Statehouse has been stripped. The Capitol lawn is a construction zone filled with materials and machines. A multiphase project that began in 2001 will continue through 2011.

It's a 100-year-old building and then some. Construction began in 1867 and was completed in 1903.

We were there on a Saturday and I was surprised to find the building open—and that a dome tour was about to start.

Last spring, Dave climbed the 296 steps on the dome tour. Dave had showed me his photographs of the uppermost staircase, which hangs 75 feet above the inner dome, and I was fairly certain in advance that I wouldn't be climbing that particular stairway.

On the tour, visitors can stop at any level they choose. I stopped at the eighth floor because that hanging stairway was the next step.

The eighth floor is above the inner dome but below the outer dome. On this level there are plenty of windows and I circled the inside of the dome to look out over Topeka.

"One hundred twenty-two steps left and you'll be there," the tour guide said to those who continued ascending.

A 4-year-old bounced up the staircase. She, her lagging father, and about seven others, including Dave, made it to the very top. They walked around outside on the tiny balcony that rims the top of the green dome, just below our silent friend, Ad Astra, and nearly 300 feet above the ground floor.

The dome tour is an adventure, but the Capitol has much more to offer: art, architecture, symbolism and history.

Renovations on the Senate chamber were completed as the 2006 legislative session began. This room is something to ooh and ahh about—the chamber is gorgeous.

Slanted November light beamed through the south windows during our tour. I felt a sense of grandeur in this hall with its ornate molding, gold leaf detail and brass pillars with morning glory and rose designs.

Our tour guide pointed out lamps in the room. "Those four lights represent eternal peace and they are always on. If you drive by at night you can see the lights through the windows," she said.

The guide also mentioned the chandelier globes, hand-crafted in Czechoslovakia. Each globe has 34 stars etched into the glass to represent Kansas as the 34th state.

A bookshelf in the Senate chamber shows off the legislators' authorship—volumes of Kansas Statutes Annotated—an anthology of laws. Not a best seller, but a fun read nonetheless.

Standing in the Statehouse rotunda are limestone statues of four famous Kansans: Dwight D. Eisenhower, Amelia Earhart, Arthur Capper and William Allen White.

Several artists have painted murals on the Statehouse walls, but the most dramatic and most recognized artwork is *Tragic Prelude,* the John Brown mural by John Steuart Curry.

On this quiet Saturday afternoon, the Statehouse was a building of closed doors, each one holding a mystery. Hallways carried the sound of museum echoes, footsteps on marble as a Capitol police officer made his rounds.

An F-5 tornado that streaked through Topeka on June 8, 1966, tore off a piece of the dome, but showed that this building will not fly away with the wind. Those acres of marble help keep it grounded.

Inside and out, the Capitol exudes strength and beauty. It is our beacon on the prairie.

June 2010

A PURE KANSAS NIGHT

"What's the story here?" I asked Dave Kendall.

"The story is the amazing ability of this place to hold off rain," he said with a smile.

Kendall, host and executive producer of KTWU's *Sunflower Journeys,* was serving as the evening's master of ceremonies. I spoke with him on June 12 about an hour before the conductor raised the baton to begin the Fifth Annual Symphony in the Flint Hills.

But the story—yes, the weather caught us all by surprise. In a good way for once.

Everyone had been watching the forecasts all week, and it was difficult to have much confidence that the clouds would be well behaved that evening. In fact, many folks had used their windshield wipers on the way to the symphony. But good weather reigned, not the skies. The day was not too hot, not too windy; it was just right.

Kansas in the springtime is like walking on a teeter-totter plank. The quality of weather can go up or down in a hurry. And perhaps the 7,000 or so folks who came to the South Clements Pasture near Bazaar simply willed away any storms.

Prior to the music, concert-goers learned about the Flint Hills from experts, many of them local residents. There were cowboys and cowgirls, poets and astronomers. Talks were given about the prairie chicken, ponds and springs, ranch horses, rodeos and cattle trails.

Governor Mark Parkinson spoke passionately about our state and proclaimed that this was "a pure Kansas night."

The Kansas City Symphony's music was as beautiful as the prairie setting. Conducted by Steven Jarvi, they began with

Gould's "Cowboy Rhapsody," followed by "Prairie Journal" by Copland. The symphony played a dozen pieces including Copland's "Buckaroo Holiday" and the themes from "Lonesome Dove" and "The Big Country."

Like the cowboys on horseback, I would've loved to have been off alone in the pastures listening to that music. And what a backdrop the land gave to the symphony.

Music swelled like the rounded hills, which were covered with rich blue-green grass and dotted by wildflowers. Above was the huge sky with its shifting clouds, and way behind the concert shell a lone horseman stood on the ridge.

Meanwhile, in the adjacent pasture, four or five cowboys rounded up cattle which had been grazing. Once gathered, the cattle seemed to know to stay put and the animals simply stood in a huddle until it was time. Then the cowboys ran the cattle up the hill behind the symphony shell. A while later, they drove a much larger herd, hundreds of head, down the hill to symphonic accompaniment. I don't suppose the cattle knew they were being used for entertainment purposes, but they provided an amazing show.

With the K.C. Symphony as his band, Lyle Lovett performed several songs: "Which Way Does That Old Pony Run," "If I Had a Boat" and "Natural Forces." And he led the audience in singing "Home on the Range."

Lovett talked about the frontier spirit, stated that "This (region) is the backbone of our country," and he seemed genuinely pleased to be in Kansas and a part of the evening.

"What an incredible feeling to stand in front of the Kansas City Symphony like this and to look out at you folks on this great prairie," Lovett said. "This is truly something I'll remember all of my life."

I think that night is something many people will hold onto.

Mr. Edward Bass, it was a pleasure to be on your land along with the few thousand folks who were lucky enough to get tickets to the event and those who served as volunteers. Gratitude goes to the K.C. Symphony for the incredible talent, and a big thank you to those who planned so well for the enjoyment of the concert-goers.

A sunset would have provided a brilliant Kansas nightcap,

but that was not to be; the sun hit the horizon behind a banner of clouds.

As the cowboys on horseback stood watch, the crowd hiked or rode to the parking lot with lightning flickering in the dark distance, and the cattle once again had the pastures to themselves.

February 2005

WHAT KANSAS KNOWS

Like many of you, I'm a Kansas lifer, a child of the prairie.

Kansas is the land where I was born, where I struggled for balance after Dad removed the training wheels from my bicycle.

Here, my brother and cousins and I dragged a mattress out of Grandma's farmhouse to fall asleep counting stars.

As Kansans, you and I can sense the line of horizon even in the dark.

We've put our faith in the change of seasons. Year after year, these winters roll over to spring. And standing in the nervous warmth of March, we scan the Flint Hills for signs of new life.

Each April, as henbit brushes a lavender wash over the fields and ditches, we're awed by the soft watercolor landscape.

In June, we watch combines churn like steamboats through a golden sea. And during August, we launch a fleet of grasshoppers with each step through dry grass.

You and I would be different people had we spent our lives gazing at Wisconsin or Wyoming skies. We would have memorized another state motto and worn winter coats on a different landscape.

In her book *Thunder and Lightning*, Natalie Goldberg writes about a Kansas woman who attended one of her writing workshops. Goldberg writes, "I had teased her several times, saying to the group, 'Find out what Kansas knows.' In truth it was I who wanted to know what she knew, living her life in one place."

So what does Kansas know? What does a person glean from living his or her entire life in this state?

I could tell Natalie Goldberg that we've swayed with the

chorus of cicadas, counted 74 shades of blue sky, and that we know every shadow of the wind.

Over the years, we've watched barns first surrender their paint. Then they lose their straight lines. Outbuildings lean, sometimes for a decade, before kneeling to the ground.

Many of us have rubbed fingers over the ribbed whiskers of wheat. And as kids, we climbed aboard Grandpa's pigeon-toed tractor and blackened our hands on its steering wheel.

Kansans are familiar with the race between a pickup and the swell of dust that chases it. The truck arrives at the stop sign first, but the dust sails victoriously through the intersection. We've swallowed that dust and have cleaned its dark clumps from the corners of our eyes. Some windy days when we wash our hair, the water turns brown.

Kansans are acquainted with the cedars that stand watch in the cemeteries and the chain-link fences that draw the graveyard's boundaries. The names carved on the granite stones are our family names. We've buried grandparents here. This is our ancestral home.

We connect ourselves to the prairie like rhizomes, laying a tendril here and there. We dig into the soil; we take nourishment from the land.

And if someday we leave the plains, we will take with us a scrapbook of images that the seasons have burned into our subconscious mind.

What does Kansas know?

We know home when we see it.

Life on the Ground

June 2007

NIK AND SAM CROSS KANSAS

Midweek, both boys crashed their bikes.

But both of them got up again. They rode every mile of BAK, Biking Across Kansas.

These boys are my nephews Nik and Sam, ages 9 and 11, from Alaska, who recently rode the 500-mile route from Tribune to Elwood in eight days. My brother, Leon, rode his bike with them and Margaret, his wife, drove their support vehicle.

On Day 7 of their journey, my mother and I caught up with them in Troy, in northeast Kansas. Team Alaska rode slower than the crowd. The Unruhs cruised into Troy that evening nearly 12 hours after their 7:34 a.m. start.

When I asked Sam about his favorite part of BAK, he replied, "Crossing the Oregon Trail," near Blue Rapids. The Oregon Trail was a recent topic in their home-schooling studies.

"The hills" were Nik's favorite part. "They're actually pretty easy if you shift into the right gear," he said.

"Near Lake Wilson, there were some monster hills. I couldn't keep up with (the boys)," Leon said. "They just decided they were going to ride and they did. These guys rode up every hill without stopping. They didn't give up anywhere."

Leon and Margaret have each biked across Kansas three times. (That's how they met in 1985.) They believe in riding on two wheels the entire route, not hitching a ride or walking their bikes up the hills.

Margaret said, "I told the boys, 'You don't walk your bike unless it's broken.'"

There were difficulties along the way. On rural pavement with a treacherous sand shoulder, both boys wrecked within a few miles of each other. Nik came through his accident relatively unscathed.

Sam, sailing 20 mph downhill, caught a tire in the loose sand and went down hard on the asphalt. His left side was bruised and bloody, with wounds to his chin, elbow, hand, hip and knee. Leon rushed to Sam, checked his injuries and comforted him.

"He got back on his bike, and we got to the next town a quarter-mile away," Leon said. "A rain came through and we had time to sit and think."

They rode another 40 miles that day.

"Now he knows he's a hero, 'cause he has his scars," Leon said, smiling.

That evening, after the BAK meeting on the Troy town square, we sat on the courthouse steps. Sam and Nik chased fireflies on the lawn.

"(On the ride) the boys smelled their first skunk," Margaret said. (Kansas roadkill differs from that in Alaska.) Among the dead animals they saw was a raccoon that had been draped with Mardi Gras beads, courtesy of another BAK rider.

Turning to me, Leon said, "It was fun, just for them to see Kansas like we did (growing up), the bad asphalt roads, the farms, the rivers."

Margaret didn't bike in this year's BAK. Instead, she handed out Gatorade, Popsicles and encouragement to Leon and the boys.

"I just get up and drive for 12 hours," Margaret laughed. One thing she enjoyed was "parking out by myself and seeing the wheat blowing around and hearing the birds."

Leon said, for him, the best part of BAK was "after Sam had his spill near Wells, that he got back on the bike."

"My absolute favorite part," he added, more seriously, "was after the spill, seeing Sam get up."

I was impressed with how Nik and Sam handled the 500-mile ride. Both boys beamed with new confidence.

The next morning, Team Alaska rode to the finish line. They dipped their bike tires into the Missouri River, signaling their successful journey across Kansas.

"They appreciated the changing landscape and learned about lending a helpful hand to others," Leon said. "They accepted the best and worst parts of BAK with equal grace."

June 2010

IN THE DIRT

When Dave Leiker was a young boy, he and his brothers eagerly explored a stream near the old farm where his family lived for a year. Like the dirt and mud that surely set into his jeans and his shirts, the love of exploring nature set into his soul.

As an adult, not much has changed. Ditches and creek banks seem to be my husband's natural habitat. He's an in-the-dirt photographer—which is why he calls his website "Prairie Dust."

The other day, headed toward Great Bend, we stopped along K-150 in Marion County so we could take pictures of wildflowers in the ditch.

"What do you like to photograph most?" I asked him.

"Just the spirit of things," he replied. "The life force."

We didn't have bug spray with us, but he spread a drop cloth so he could avoid some of the chiggers and he sprawled out to take photos of a swaying clump of black-eyed Susans.

Dave explained the process. "Now, I'll shoot into the light. They'll be backlit so the light comes through and really illuminates them."

"I'm always watching the histogram," he said. "Catching details and highlights in the blossoms and yet keeping texture in the sky—it's almost impossible to do both."

"Up close you see all the pinholes from where the bugs have eaten," he said. "This is so much more interesting to me than a domestic garden because of the wildness and the textures."

Dave and I stopped later near Ellinwood. As he wandered in the ditch, I took photos of the adjacent wheat field. When he returned, there were 10 mosquitoes riding his back.

As we drove off, hot and sweaty and bug bitten, he said, "That's the price of admission: chiggers, mosquitoes, and the occasional tick. But it's worth it. That's why I get the photos that other people don't—they have more sense than I do."

Dave often returns from photography trips with a sweat-drenched shirt, a water line on his jeans and mud on his back pockets. I imagine his mother had to deal with similar laundry issues.

One day in May, Dave came home beaming after a morning on horseback, having photographed Ryan Arndt and a crew of cowboys in Chase County as they rounded up cattle and worked the calves.

The Flint Hills had woken up with fog and Dave brought home dozens of incredible photos. He created an electronic slide show set to music. Both the slide show and a number of prints were on display, along with work from other photographers, at the Symphony in the Flint Hills Gallery in Cottonwood Falls during the rodeo and symphony weekends.

When I met Dave 19 years ago, he wouldn't have anything to do with cameras. He had kept his Nikon from his days as a portrait photographer in Salina, but he didn't use it. He was burned out from shooting countless portraits and weddings.

It wasn't until Dave created our website (FlyoverPeople.net) in 2004 that he got back into photography—digital, this time. I bought myself a little Canon Elph, and exploring Kansas together with cameras is something we've done with gusto ever since.

In addition to being a whiz kid with photography, Dave is also a computer genius. He works as Web and Media Manager for the Emporia school district.

While many folks are enamored of his landscape photos, which capture the dramatic and diverse moods of Kansas, it's those weed, grass and wildflower shots that Dave enjoys most.

"I put on a clean pair of jeans the other day and they still had grass stains on the knees. It's kind of like being a painter," he said, pleased that the effort of his work remained as a badge of identification.

To view Dave's photos, check out www.FlyoverPeople.net/galleries.htm.

May 2003

AIN'T THAT EMPORIA

It's the way the stoplights on Sixth Avenue glow at dusk, the luminous row of red and green that steals attention from the creamy blue sky.

That's Emporia. To me, anyway.

That is home.

A thousand things can turn a town into a hometown. Perhaps it's the five maples in front of Emporia Fitness, each one changing its autumn colors at a different pace. Or the great blue heron hiding behind cattails in the C of E pond. Maybe it's the weathered stone at the Peter Pan Park amphitheater.

Emporia means eating barbecue at Bobby D's, dining on steak at Bruff's and reading the daily "Good Evening" in *The Gazette*.

My husband and I once considered leaving Emporia. Had we moved, I would miss friends, of course, but also other people who make a town feel like home: the chiropractor who knows where each of my bones belongs; the mechanic who performed a miracle on my starter; a friendly banker; a trustworthy lawyer.

Sometimes it's trial and error finding the right person for the job; usually it's word of mouth. But once you find them, you keep them. They become like extended family.

For as long as I've been the one responsible for my own tire care, I've taken my wheels to Mel Reed. After years of working for another dealer, last year he opened his own business, Mel's Tire.

Recently, I visited Mel with my squealing brakes. While Doyle Kirby repaired the brakes, I watched Mel greet each customer by name.

Thirteen years ago, when my Toyota was new, I told Mel I wanted to buy a full-sized spare and a wheel to put it on. The donut tire made me nervous. I'd prefer a real tire, I said.

Mel asked, "On your Mazda, how many miles did you put on that spare?"

"About five."

"Don't waste your money," he said. "You don't need a new tire. You'll be fine."

And Mel was right; my four tires (several sets of them) have held their air quite well.

That's only one reason I followed Mel to his new shop. Besides not selling you something you don't need, Mel is so likable that you wish he were a relative, someone to sit down with at Thanksgiving dinner.

Good people live all over this town. I'm sure that the other tire dealers are pleasant and respectable; I just happened to find Mel first.

Emporia has been my home for more than 20 years. I'll admit that for a long time I saw Emporia as just another flat city. Ordinary. Plain. OK, I'll say it: boring. But Emporia is a nice town.

It will never be as energetic and quaint as Lawrence and we're without the country-club shopping of Kansas City. We don't have Wichita's Indian and Thai restaurants or the coveted Target that Topeka has, but we can zip to these cities in 90 minutes or less.

Upon our return from a long trip, Emporia feels fresh and unfamiliar. You've observed other parts of the country through vacation eyes and when you drive back into town, there it is – the S & S Café. The slanted windows and the neon lines haven't changed, but now it looks striking, artsy, like a setting for a movie.

Surprisingly, this is home.

Barbara Kingsolver said, "I've spent hundreds of pages, even whole novels, trying to explain what home means to me. Sometimes, I think it is the only thing I ever write about."

Maybe it's the only thing any of us write about.

By living here, I've found that ordinary isn't such a bad thing, that personal service still exists, and that neighbors are so responsible that they try to resuscitate your dying goldfish while you're on vacation.

What matters, when you get down to it, is not what brings you to this town; it's what happens when you stay put.

June 2003

HANGIN' WITH LOUIS AND STAN

"That board Louis is on is very wobbly," a woman said as she stood in the parking lot, looking up at the scaffolding.

"We do that just to show off," Stan joked.

Louis moved with confidence 10 feet above the pavement while the end of the piece of lumber he stood on bounced like a diving board.

These are not just any two guys throwing paint on the building at Sixth and Merchant, but two of the finest artists Kansas has produced: Stan Herd and Louis Copt.

They had been working on the mural off and on for several weeks when I met them. I spent an hour or so hanging out with these painters as they shaped and shaded the underbelly of storm clouds on their Flint Hills scene.

When I had pulled into the parking lot, I first sat on the trunk of my car, taking notes. "Are you a painter?" Stan asked.

"No, a writer." Stan, Louis and I talked awhile and I signed their guest book.

"Would you like to come up?" Stan offered.

"Really?" I asked, delighted at the invitation.

"This must keep you in shape," I said, finding my way up the scaffold.

"This is getting me in shape," Stan said.

I climbed 12 feet to one of the metal-reinforced, nonwobbly boards and bent an elbow around a diagonal pipe for balance, leaving hands free to take notes. But I put the notebook in a pocket when Louis handed me a brush and pointed at a cloud.

"Here. Paint some—right there. Then you can say you painted on it."

"And you can paint over it if I goof it up?" I asked.

Louis smiled.

"I've painted this thing three times," Louis said, playfully dabbing his brush at a blue-violet-colored knob sticking out of the wall. "I'm not painting it again."

Stan climbed down to answer his cell phone and then stepped back for a look. "Louie, that looks great!" he shouted as he returned to the wall.

"Louie, that's kickin', baby. I like that transition. Now we pop those (high)lights in, and it's really gonna . . . ," Stan said.

"Yeah," Louis agreed.

"We need a little action in there. Sometimes you see those rolling clouds and there's this pocket . . . ," Stan said.

"How do you keep your paint from getting muddy?" I asked, as Stan sloshed paint from one container to another.

"We want it muddy. Grays make the highlights bounce," he said.

A cloud dripped. "Whoops, that's not supposed to be," Stan said as he swooped in to cover the purple drip, stretching the cloud.

"The hardest thing about doing this," Louis confided, "is smelling the barbecue," nodding his head toward Bobby D's across the street as meaty smoke drifted by.

Down on the ground, the bed of the pickup truck was their palette: open buckets of acrylic latex paint. Blues and purples, mostly. Several brushes soaked in blue-gray water.

"That is an evening primrose," Stan said, lifting a droopy yellow blossom from a plastic cup. "And this is a prairie rose. We picked them this morning on the way down here." Louis and Stan drive in from Lawrence.

Stan poured some water from the primrose's cup into a paint can to keep the paint from drying.

A worn copy of *Roadside Wildflowers of the Southern Great Plains* was lodged in the corner of the truck's dashboard.

"I'm wondering what this will look like in February, when there's snow on the ground," Louis said, contemplating their green landscape.

They expect the mural, *Spring in the Flint Hills,* to hold up for 8 to 10 years. The colors will fade, but the artists are willing to return to brighten them.

"We're having fun doing this," Stan said. "And we still like each other."

December 2007

LAURA'S CHRISTMAS COOKIES

In previous Novembers, a box from Texas always arrived at the home of Will and Laura Stibal. The box, sent by daughter Judy, contained a variety of nuts for Laura to use in the annual baking-of-the-Christmas-cookies. Laura measured and stirred pecan and walnut pieces into the countless batches of cookies that she made every December.

This year is different. And sad. The Stibals are missing their shining star; Laura passed away on September 30. She was 87.

Laura was my friend, and on visits to the Stibal home in Decembers past, I spent time with her in the kitchen. I'd help by pulling hot cookies from the oven and scooting them onto cooling racks.

She'd insist I sample each kind. (Not that I minded, mind you.)

"Have you tried one of these Russian tea cakes yet?" she'd ask.

So then I'd have my fifth cookie of the afternoon.

As a cookie connoisseur, I can say with complete confidence that Laura was one of the finest bakers of homemade goodness on the planet.

Laura spent her last couple of years in a wheelchair. Weakened by Parkinson's disease, she had trouble standing. The illness slowed her down, but it didn't stop her from baking.

It was difficult for her to maneuver the wheelchair. Just for her to get an egg from the refrigerator may have taken five minutes. But Laura had the kind of patience that you'd expect from a mother of nine. Occasionally, she'd express frustration that her body wouldn't cooperate, but I never heard any bitterness. Laura was a woman of faith, a woman of quiet strength.

Last year, I helped her make a batch of peanut brittle, my

first attempt at candy-making. Laura sat nearby and guided me. I stirred, watched the thermometer, and added the peanuts, vanilla and baking soda. At her direction, I removed the pan from the stove. Then she and Will and I, armed with greased spoons, hurriedly spread out the liquid mixture on cookie sheets until the candy hardened and we could spread no more.

Laura often talked about her Minnesota childhood as she dropped spoonfuls of sticky dough onto cookie sheets.

These were just everyday stories she told—about going ice fishing with her dad, or that she was a pretty good basketball player. I heard about one time when she and her father walked from their home on the outskirts of town into St. Cloud so he could buy her a new blouse.

She mentioned the days in the 1940s when Will was off to war. And her eyes always sparkled as she talked about her kids when they were young. "I loved those babies," she said.

Many of Laura's favorite cookie recipes were included in a family cookbook compiled several years ago by granddaughter Kelly. But I'd often find Laura thumbing through a half-dozen other cookbooks, searching for that one elusive cookie recipe she wanted to make.

When company stopped in, they were offered chocolate crinkles, ginger creams, peanut butter, or sour cream cookies. There were always peppernuts, mint surprises and the easy and festive no-bake green wreaths.

Green wreaths—Melt the following over hot water: 40 marshmallows, 1 stick margarine, lots of green food coloring. Pour mixture over 8 cups of cornflakes. Form into small wreaths and decorate with red hots.

In her last years, age and disease didn't stop Laura from stirring together sugar and flour and eggs. The cookies were a tangible expression of love. Those days in the Stibal kitchen are now treasured memories. Her cookies were the best, but it's Laura I miss—her stories, her bright spirit, her kind heart.

September 2009

TALLGRASS EXPRESS STRING BAND

That Annie Wilson, she can write some songs. If you want to understand life in the Flint Hills, then she's your gal.

Annie gets her inspiration when she pulls on her boots and steps out her back door onto the family ranch near Elmdale—where lyrics and melodies apparently fall from the clear blue sky.

Living the life of a cowgirl (and English teacher), she lets nothing in the natural world get past her. She has written a love song to tallgrass, "Big Bluestem: The King of the Prairie," and one to the prairie chicken (and the killdeer, meadowlark, red-tailed hawk . . .) in "Sail the Summer Sky." In "Kaw Trail," she tells the tribe's story: "On westward we go toward the last buffalo. . . ."

For five years, Annie Wilson has played American roots music in the Tallgrass Express String Band with Charlie Laughridge of Council Grove and Loren Ratzloff from Canton. The Tallgrass Express String Band has plenty of strings. Annie sticks with guitar; Charlie plays fiddle, mandolin, concertina and harmonica; and Loren picks up the banjo, mandolin and dobro.

The band performs at events across the region, playing about once a week during the warm months. On September 12, Dave and I watched the band perform in Cottonwood Falls.

I had been anticipating an outdoor concert and had pictured myself sitting in a folding chair on the brick street in front of the Emma Chase Café as birds swirled overhead in the darkening sky. However, the clouds held unanswered questions, so the concert was moved inside the old city auditorium.

I sensed a strong camaraderie among the three musicians and heard it in the harmony of voices and instruments. The performance was a transfer of energy, each song a gift to the audience. During one piece, I glanced over my shoulder and saw that every face in the room had a smile.

They played a couple of Charlie Laughridge's instrumentals, "Coming Home from the Z-Bar" and "Scuffalong," as well as traditional tunes and music by current artists.

As a lyrics hound, I'm taken by Annie's original songs. One of her beauties is "Clean Curve of Hill Against Sky." That title was inspired by Zula Bennington Greene's preface to *Chase County Historical Sketches, Vol. 2.* Annie begins that song with:

As we hop on our ponies to climb up the hill
While the morning breeze sleeps and air is so still
We see up ahead in the early half light
That clean curve of hill against sky.

To introduce another tune, she said that various regions of the country have homesick songs and she thought there ought to be one about being homesick for the Flint Hills. So she wrote "The Moon Can Take Me Home," which includes these lines:

I remember how the sunset fills the prairie
And coyotes sing the evening hills to sleep
As the meadowlark's sweet cry seems to linger in the sky
Till the moonlight gives the Earth a silver sheen.

The song takes us through the seasons in the Flint Hills and we, too, understand the longing we would feel if we were far from home.

After the concert, I asked Annie where she writes—indoors or out.

"I write them when I'm walking my dog," she said. "It's the rhythm. With walking you can do 3/4 time or 4/4."

"It's a little obsession right now in my life," Annie said with a grin. "I've written 20 more songs—and I have all these ideas—but we just can't play them all.

"These guys are great," she said with a nod toward Loren and Charlie. "And they're very supportive."

This band is the real deal. Their music rises from the land they love.

It's a joy to hear Loren and Charlie stir up the strings. Add Annie's lyrics about horses and coyotes, sunsets, green pastures and still morning air and, well, we just can't help but fall in love with the Flint Hills—all over again.

April 2007

AT THE BREADBASKET

The wait in the German buffet line was about 15 minutes, but I didn't mind leaning on one leg then the other for a short while—because freshly cooked verenike was up for grabs.

Returning home from the Cosmosphere in Hutchinson earlier this month, Dave and I stopped at the Breadbasket Restaurant, 219 North Main, in Newton. This restaurant serves German food on Friday and Saturday evenings.

Oh, the choices: zwieback or whole wheat bread, butter or apple butter, fried potatoes or hot German potato salad?

Except for the sauerkraut, which I could live all of my days without, the entire buffet looked delicious. I can personally vouch for the goodness of the sausage, chicken borscht and verenike with ham gravy.

OK, now I was raised in a German Mennonite community and to my recollection, in my 18 years of living there, only once was I fed borscht and moos. And I had never even heard of verenike or bohne beroggi.

How could this be? Other Kansas Mennonite communities consider these dishes to be traditional food. The German/Russian delicacies are a hit to thousands of folks at the Mennonite Central Committee Relief Sale held each April in Hutchinson. And on certain days of the week, these German dishes can also be found at restaurants in Hillsboro and Inman, Moundridge and Buhler.

The church I attended near Pawnee Rock was something of a Mennonite outpost. In Barton County, we were flung far from the McPherson, Marion and Harvey County communities where a majority of the Mennonite/Russian immigrants settled in the 1870s.

So anyway, I'm wondering, did the group of Pawnee Rock

Mennonites leave Russia in such a hurry that they forgot to grab the family recipes?

Maybe as my ancestors moved around on the open prairie near Pawnee Rock and Dundee, their cookbooks bounced off the wagons and the pages blew away with the Kansas wind.

Or perhaps my kinfolk merely assimilated too well, chucking the verenike and the borscht in favor of pan-fried chicken.

I can't complain; I ate satisfying meals at church and in the farmhouses of the elders—those second-generation Americans, the bilingual ones who often spoke Low German to one another.

Like many Americans, my tribe tends to be a meat-and-potatoes-and-bread people. As a youngster, I saw bread at every meal. If there were no rolls, I'd find white bread stacked on a plate. And at gatherings, we'd often have orange Jell-O topped with shredded carrots. (Jell-O, as you know, is the first sign of assimilation.)

No, I don't know why I was never exposed to verenike, but I have grown to really like this doughy food, which is categorized as a dumpling. It's filled with dry cottage cheese, boiled, then sometimes fried in a skillet to add crispy texture. It is served with ham gravy.

For dessert at the Breadbasket, I passed by the German chocolate cake, the cherry moos and the cookies, selecting the bohne beroggi, which is a food that confounds me, actually. The first time I tried this dessert, it just seemed bizarre to me that anyone would think to put refried beans into a sweet bread dough, bake it, then drench it in a sweet sauce.

I found a recipe for bohne beroggi on the Internet. There's cream in the dough and in the sweetened, mashed pinto beans, and the sauce includes half-and-half. No wonder they're yummy.

My own kin failed to feed me bohne beroggi and verenike, but when I eat this food I feel like a sturdy German. Sauerkraut aside, it's all good stuff.

February 2009

RECALCULATING

We've just met, but I think Daniel may hate me already.

Daniel is the voice in our new Global Positioning System unit.

So far this guy has kept his emotions in check, but I'm not sure how long that will last—he might turn on me.

UPS delivered the GPS last week. It's a gift from my mother. We're planning a trip in which Dave and I will meet Mom along the Buffalo River in Arkansas. She thought we'd enjoy having an electronic navigation system for those unfamiliar roads in the Ozarks.

Dave and I took our maiden voyage with the GPS unit recently when we headed for Great Bend.

The device has dozens of languages available. Because Dave and I don't speak fluent Srpski, Eesti, Hrvatski or even Letzebuergesch, we decided on plain old English. Well, plain old English with a twist of lime.

"Let's use the guy with a British accent," I told Dave. He poked around on the touch-screen and that's how Daniel came into our lives.

Thanks to the magic of electronics, triangulation and satellites, our little GPS unit knows exactly where we are and lays out the road before us, revealing curves, speed limits, and naming crossroads.

"Does it show deer in the ditches, or do I still have to watch for them?" I asked Dave.

A purple path represents the roadway on the screen. When there's a turn ahead, a white arrow appears and Daniel will give us a verbal heads-up.

The screen shows your estimated arrival time, the speed of

your car and also, in most places, the speed limit of the highway. When we came over the hill into Strong City, as soon as we crossed into the 45 mph zone, the GPS noted the change.

I don't need satellites to find Great Bend. After 28 years of driving between Emporia and Barton County, I could probably drive there with my eyes closed. Great Bend is due west of Emporia. There's really only one reasonable way to get there: U.S. 50 to K-150 to U.S. 56. Except for a few curves and veering to the right onto K-150 near Elmdale, you seldom use the steering wheel on this route.

But Daniel, well, he came up with an out-of-the-way way to get to Great Bend.

As we passed Elmdale, I asked Dave, "Shouldn't this thing be telling us to turn onto K-150?"

The GPS was silent. The screen indicated we should stay on U.S. 50.

I wasn't going to let Daniel steer me wrong. I turned onto K-150. Daniel said, "Recalculating," and there was a pause. Then, "Turn left in .2 miles on an unpaved road."

Daniel wanted us to be on U.S. 50. Very much so. He kept recalculating, kept trying to realign us. He urged us to see the error of our ways, bless his little electronic heart.

Later, in McPherson, Dave and I wanted to photograph the old opera house and I turned on Main Street. Daniel immediately began his "recalculating" shtick. I then made several more "wrong" turns. On each one Daniel jumped in with his British-accented "recalculating, recalculating," and "turn left in .1 mile," trying desperately to get us back on the straight and narrow.

Each time he corrected us, I could picture the guy rolling his eyes, sighing at my driving disobedience.

This GPS is a great new toy, but we need to learn how to better program it so that Daniel doesn't fry a circuit in one of his recalculating frenzies.

Actually, it was kind of fun to see if I could shake up Daniel, get him off his game. Yeah, he's gonna hate me. And when he does, there are other GPS voices to turn to; I'll bet that Lee has a lovely Australian accent.

July 2009

WE KAN—AND WE ARE

It was a Kansas moment, one that made me feel flat-out proud.

I stood inside the Whiting Café, watching new windows go in, the ceiling being painted, the stove being degreased. Nearly everything had been removed from the building; volunteers were renovating the 25-seat restaurant in the Jackson County town of Whiting (pop. 206).

This was the pilot project of We Kan, part of the Kansas Sampler Foundation. We Kan is a group of Kansans working together to find ways to keep their small communities and hometown businesses viable.

On a hot summer morning, about 40 people, most of them strangers to one another, worked side by side. I observed kindness, laughter, teamwork, camaraderie. It was well worth the 90-minute drive to Whiting just to absorb that positive energy.

In this world, some people are naysayers; they stand around, kick the dirt and mutter things like, "We can't," or "There's no money for this project" or "It's not our problem."

On the flip side, the Whiting Café, dismantled and in disarray, was filled with purposeful activity and, well, joy.

At the makeover site hung a "We Kan!" banner. Beneath "We Kan!" someone had posted a sticker with the handwritten words, "And we are."

Many of these workers had never been to Whiting before and didn't personally know Rosa Thomas, the café's owner. But they heard the call for help and came to refurbish the restaurant. During the weekend of June 26–28 about 100 people showed up in work clothes.

Kansas Sampler Foundation director Marci Penner said that as volunteers appeared, they sorted themselves out: "I'm a window guy." "I'm a floor guy." "I'm a cabinet guy."

"It's a great combination of skilled people and hard workers," Penner said.

As I spoke with her, men built shelves, a woman defrosted a freezer, others planted flowers outside beneath a snazzy new mural that proclaims "Food so great, you'll scrape your plate."

Five thousand dollars was raised for the project. "Everyone gets turned on by how they can help," Penner said. "Some by sending in $5, others by volunteering."

The Whiting Café project was the first transaction of the We Kan Bank, a social capital experiment. The We Kan Bank plans to have a website in which volunteer-led communities can open "accounts of need" and others can open "accounts of support," offering services, skills or money.

Penner said that through the We Kan Bank, a family or group could find a project that fits their skill level, contact that community and help make it happen. And, once a year or so, the We Kan group will likely host a major "I Kan Help" project such as the Whiting Café makeover.

"Deciding on Rosa was one of those serendipitous things," Penner said. "Rosa called me and invited me to her café's 25th anniversary in August."

Penner had a calendar conflict and couldn't attend, but then the idea to renovate the restaurant popped into her head.

"We're not a government agency," Penner said. "There's no red tape. I can just send out an e-blast (to We Kan and Kansas Explorers Club members) and the next minute the project is underway."

"The amazing thing is that Rosa never asked for any of this. She just got chosen," Penner wrote to volunteers after the event. "Rosa and her café got picked because anyone who can keep a restaurant open for 25 years in a town of 200 deserves a prize. This was her prize."

On makeover day, I located Rosa Thomas at the Whiting community center. She and other local women were preparing lunch for the volunteers. Thomas was and is, as you might expect, overwhelmed by the enormous gift. When I mentioned the goodhearted nature of the workers, she agreed: "Aren't they nice? They're so beautiful."

Yes, beautiful, hardworking and generous. For many of the volunteers, fixing up the Whiting Café will have no direct benefit for them—they just wanted to help, to be of service. A perfect Kansas moment, indeed.

Seasons

April 2003

EMPORIA, TURNED INSIDE OUT

A block south of my front porch, a Harley-Davidson idles. After a minute of shaking that air space, it wanders up the street toward me.

I close my eyes. The quake pulses with my blood, a lost memory echoes in my soul. Home has found me.

The low rumble of the motorcycle is as primal as a mother's heartbeat thumping on the womb. As the Harley thunders by, my eyes open and it ain't Momma I see, but a heavy-set biker with a coarse-haired ponytail and green tattoos dripping off his thick and yeasty arm.

Forget robins. Harleys are the first sure sign of spring.

We've spent months locked inside the sensory deprivation chamber of winter. I've watched the silent cold neighborhood from the windows of my living room. The extra glass of the storm windows mutes street sounds and train whistles. Winter freezes the usual sweet aromas from the bakery, the sour smells of the meat-packing plant.

On the first decent weekend of the year, I step from my living room isolation booth onto the front porch where a world of noise chatters in the air.

Emporia vibrates with sound. Kids' voices squeal and shout. From a neighbor's garage, a power saw whines, a hammer bangs. Downtown at Fire Station No. 1, a siren jumps off the starting line and heads west on Sixth Street. The scream of the ambulance scars the air and separates the winners from the losers.

The entire neighborhood has received the same message: everyone is outdoors. My husband prunes the hedge. Wayne rakes his yard. Teenage boys across the street toss a football. Two trendy middle school-aged girls walk by, practically marching because of their clunky black shoes with inflexible 3-inch soles.

Sitting on my porch steps, greasy with sunblock, I absorb the full blast of sunshine. The heat sinks through my T-shirt and soothes skin and bones that haven't really been warm since September. Sunlight beams gently onto my face, caressing it with soft brush strokes. Too much sun can kill you, but my opinion is that not enough sunlight can be just as deadly.

This is a grand reunion with my long-lost friend, Mr. Sun. It is a purification ceremony, as if the sun can burn away the shadows that have taken up residence in my thoughts during winter's long confinement.

A jogger runs down the street chased by last year's autumn leaves which skitter and scrape on the asphalt. The pin oaks look forlorn as they stubbornly cling to withered leaves, brown tears refusing to fall. On the sycamore tree next door, seed pods dangle from branches. These chestnut-colored pods are like tiny alien planets, pitted and spiked.

"Aw, aw," a crow calls. Dogs carry on conversations between alley pens, gossiping nonstop, although they've had all winter to exchange stories.

Eminem chants a slow rhythm: "Du-du-du-DU, du-du-du-DU." His voice emanates from a black Subaru with a scruffy mutt hanging out the passenger-side window. I sometimes get a little behind on listening to rap music, but I'll be caught up by the end of summer. A pickup truck piping out the party sound of salsa music dances down the street.

Neighbor girls, with whom I've shared only shivering hellos during the past five months, stroll over to my porch where I'm reading the newspaper. The girls have grown since October. Between the two of them, ages 7 and 4, they ask 17 questions: "Why does this chair rock, but not this one?" "What's Dave doing?" "Do you want to buy a candle?"

As I attempt to answer the questions that are piling up on me, a motorcycle obliterates the song of birds. The noise stops our conversation and we turn toward the street.

For just a moment, I reconnect with that holy heartbeat as the Harley rumbles by.

April 2003

LIVING IN THE ALLEY

"Californians think our lives are constantly in danger," my friend Janet, a former Californian, told me one day as we discussed tornadoes. "They think our lives are continually disrupted by weather, that we're always having tornadoes or else snow so deep we can't get out the door."

That's funny, because that's how I picture the people of California: repeatedly tormented by mudslides, wildfires and earthquakes. When I think of natural calamities and acts of God, I think California.

People become accustomed to the weather dangers in their area. Kansans coexist with tornadoes. The East and Gulf coasts accept that their ocean views invite hurricanes, and Californians adapt to tremors, aware that "the big one" may be on its way.

As catastrophes go, I'll stick with tornadoes, thank you. One can duck and cover when a twister spins into her neighborhood, but with an earthquake, there are no escape routes. And hurricanes bring that tedious week of indecision while the storm debates where to make landfall.

With spring upon us, Emporia tests tornado sirens every Wednesday at 10 a.m. Some years, that's the only time we hear them. Other years, it can be every night for a week that the sirens order us to "Take cover NOW."

Kansans scan the clouds when the day boils over. We measure the sky and gauge the probability of disaster. Before we go underground, we want to face our assailant.

On June 7, 1990, as an evening storm approached Emporia, I stood on my front porch and watched the southwestern view fill with impending doom. Green, yellow, purple, black. The sky was alive. And it was not in a good mood.

The bungalow on Lawrence Street that I rented had no basement, only a spider-infested crawl space.

Some experts suggest that people whose homes have no basements could hide in a bathtub and pull a mattress or something solid over themselves for protection from flying debris. I had an iron claw-foot bathtub, but couldn't quite muscle that old waterbed mattress up and out of the bed frame.

As I watched from my porch, a black funnel formed in the western sky, beyond the town's beef packing plant. Jeff O'Dell, Emporia's ever-present newscaster, announced the storm's play-by-play over the radio.

When the tornado siren paused for breath, my new neighbor, who had been observing the sky from her house across the street, yelled at me, "Do you have a basement?"

"No," I shouted back, glancing at the vertical cloud that seemed to be jogging in place.

"Do you want to come over?" she asked.

"Yeah, I do," I replied. Better safe than dead.

I sat out the storm in a basement with neighbors, listening to their radio and their wailing baby. Static crackled over the airwaves. Jeff O'Dell eventually relayed the "all clear."

Although the tornado had left town, Emporia was not all clear.

The twister rearranged the western edge of Emporia, chewing up dozens of homes and businesses and flipping cars at John North Ford. About 20 people were hurt, at least two of them seriously. Some people's lives changed abruptly.

The tragedy didn't play long in this venue. Our happy-go-lucky sky betrayed us, but the wounds inflicted became badges of survival and strength.

While visiting with my Uncle Jay, whose home is hidden in the Arkansas hills, I mentioned that with all those trees, they couldn't possibly see storms and tornadoes approach. Jay replied, "It keeps you from having to worry about them."

A psychic reads palms, but our future is told in the clouds. It is our habit to survey the heavens, to see what's up there. Because once in a while, the sky tumbles to earth.

And where it does, it leaves a thousand tales.

July 2008

STORM SEASON

Outsiders sometimes ask me, "What's there to do in Kansas?"

Considering the recent springtime weather, I think I could honestly respond: "Well, we Kansans spend a lot of our time dodging hailstones."

As of this writing, Emporia has avoided the large hail, but many parts of the state have been pelted with icy stones the size of golfballs, baseballs, even softballs.

This spring our sky has been an overachiever. Day after day, thunderstorms have tumbled across Kansas, throwing hail, dropping rain and spinning the occasional tornado. Those twisters have killed residents, smashed barns and homes, and paid unwelcome visits to a number of places, including Manhattan and Chapman.

Actually, the state has had more than the occasional tornado. As of June 16, preliminary reports indicated that Kansas had experienced 172 tornadoes so far in 2008. Our yearly average is 55. In that June 16 news story, Iowa came in second with 134 twisters; Missouri had 127.

Those yellow, orange and red blobs on the TV weather maps have been out to get us. Each evening, we've watched the dancing colors on the radar screen. We're certainly getting our money's worth out of the meteorologists this year.

Nearly every day during the past two months, my Internet browser has displayed a weather alert symbol. Sometimes that red octagon has announced a thunderstorm warning, sometimes a flash flood watch or a wind advisory.

Weatherwise, Kansas can be an exciting place. But over the years, we've been astonished by the weather so many times that anymore there's nothing the sky can throw down that will surprise us.

Highway crews can be plowing through a blizzard in western Kansas, and on the same day eastern Kansas residents are fighting off of a herd of stampeding tornadoes.

Springtime in the Sunflower State—it is the best of times; it is the worst of times. Kansas is the poster state for mood swings. There's that oft-repeated saying around here, "If you don't like the weather, wait five minutes . . . it'll get worse."

A stagnant weather pattern? Well, that comes in August when meteorologists don't even bother to show up for work. The TV stations replay the same forecast ad nauseam: hot, hazy, humid, 94 degrees.

As for living with the threat of tornadoes, that's just part of being a Kansan. We take the black funnels in stride. There's a certain amount of pride and bravado that comes from living on this land where danger hangs in the air.

On a June evening when the sirens sounded in Emporia, if there had been a visitor from California here, he might have thought we were under an earthquake warning because people rushed out onto their front lawns. We gawked at the sky and talked on cell phones. Of course, instead, we all should've been racing down the basement stairs and diving under a sturdy table.

Many of us want to watch tornadoes and photograph them. However, the odds of actually being in the same place at the same time as a tornado aren't all that great. And some of those tornadoes are rain-wrapped, shrouded and therefore not visible.

Simon, an e-mail friend in England, once asked, "Have you seen a twister? Do flyover people grow up with this ever-present danger ('Sorry I'm late for school, Miss; we hit some trouble and my homework's in Texas')—or is it very rare?"

Yep, Simon, I've seen seven or eight tornadoes in my lifetime, but have never lost my homework, or anything else, to a twister.

Living on the plains though, we take our chances. Our landscape and location invite the massive thunderstorms, the hail, the tornadoes—and all we can do is ride out each storm.

A Kansan gets used to living with the Jekyll-and-Hyde skies. Storms are just part of our nature.

November 2005

NOT EVEN ON THE MAP

We've got trees, by golly.

Lots of them, actually.

Well, OK, Kansas doesn't have quite as many trees as, say, Tennessee or Arkansas, or maybe even the tiny state of Vermont. Still, I'm a little disappointed that Kansas is not even on the map when The Weather Channel draws its fall foliage lines.

The Weather Channel's Web site has a map of the United States that shows where to find the peak of autumn color. According to them, Kansas doesn't have a peak.

While much of the United States map is happily smeared in yellow or orange or red, revealing the passage of color north to south, about 98 percent of Kansas shows up as gray-green, a non-color. Only a tiny strip along the Missouri border indicates any foliage in the Sunflower State.

Kansas is not alone. For a large portion of the central states, from South Dakota to Texas, autumn shades simply don't exist on The Weather Channel's map.

Apparently our area isn't fluffy enough to pull in travelers. Fine. That means more leaves for the rest of us.

Even if Kansas doesn't attract the autumn tour buses, our leaves do sign off with a splash of color just like everyone else's. Brilliant maples remind me of the old Trix cereal commercials: "Raspberry red, orange orange, lemon yellow."

Of course, wind rattles the maples and the cottonwoods. Leaves drop. Now, what do we do with them?

Lawnmowers grind and chew. Power blowers whine every weekend. Leaves are raked up, scraped up, sucked up, blown away. They are saved as mulch, stuffed into bags, dumped into trailers, hauled to the landfill.

I miss the fragrance of burning leaves. A lot of things that can be burned don't have a pleasant odor. Leaves do. I was a leaf burner back in the days when backyard fires were an everyday event inside the city limits of Pawnee Rock.

In fact, as a child fascinated with matches, my favorite chore was burning the trash. In the back yard, beyond the swing set, sat a rusty, 55-gallon drum in which I burned the Campbell's soup cans, Lucky Charms cereal boxes and Columbia Record Club junk mail.

Rainbo bread wrappers dissolved at the touch of a match. The plastic bags shriveled into a fragile black curl. It was at this trash barrel that I discovered what toxic odors are all about. And I learned to step out of the wind.

So, in those days of backyard burning, we often set fire to the thick-veined elm leaves that fell on the front lawn. Thick smoke spewed from the volcano of leaves.

Leaf raking was another favorite chore—but, again, only because there was something in it for me. I'd take a running start and roll into the pile of leaves. But, no matter how huge I made the heap, the ground was still hard beneath it.

As I ran and jumped, I always thought of a line from a Peanuts cartoon. I believe it was Linus who stated the obvious, something like: "Never jump into a pile of leaves while holding a wet sucker."

My days of jumping into mounds of crispy leaves are over. But it is autumn again, and my front yard crunches, thanks in large part to leaves donated by the neighbor's sycamore.

Trees? Leaves? Kansas has plenty. And the proof is piling up around us.

November 2007

CHASING THE LIGHT

Once again, we've tricked the sun into rising an hour earlier.

Yes, we are the jugglers of time; we can reschedule the sun. Well, actually, it's not we little people who boss the sun around; light-shifting takes an act of Congress.

But if not for the dramatic time change recently, we might not have realized that darkness has crept into our lives. A few minutes here and there we don't notice, but when night lurches forward an entire hour, that gets our attention.

Yes, we've replaced our smoke alarm batteries and rolled back our clocks to Central Standard Time. Now, at 5:30 p.m., night pours through our windows.

Many Kansans enjoy these cold months and the darkness and mysteries held within; for them, this is the cozy season. Some welcome November because the night air carries the drift of wood smoke from neighbors' chimneys. There's the fleet of honking geese overhead and the crisp outline of stars.

And sometimes I let myself go that way too, surrendering to November, letting the darkness seep into my skin, allowing the night to take me over. I suppose that's the best way to be, to ride with the seasons rather than fight them.

But living in the dark goes against my blood: I am a light chaser. And when the evenings were stolen by the dark, I did what came naturally: I bought another lamp, a floor lamp, to dispel the darkness.

Now, I'm not afraid of the dark; I am a collector of light, a light freak. There are people who require chocolate; well, I need light. I tend to fall in line with German philosopher Johann Wolfgang von Goethe, whose last words were: "More light!"

Darkness seems to control the fall and winter seasons, but if light and dark were, say, arm wrestling, darkness would hit the table with a thud, because light is the stronger of the two powers.

In the Kansas skies at night, the tiny blinking lights on airplanes can be seen all the way from the ground. And take the stars that hang in galaxies light-years away—one might think that the rays of those stars would be swallowed up by millions and millions of miles and the blackness of space, yet those distant stars are visible to us. Light wins again.

Sunlight is powerful, but it's not always direct or intense. Daylight is in short supply for the next few months while our sun sizzles over Brazil. We may be able to manipulate the sun's hours, but we cannot force it to provide more light.

In the early afternoons when autumn's shadows fall into my house and the sunlight is as thin as skim milk, my thoughts turn to lamps and lights and 150-watt bulbs.

Now I seldom turn on more than 11 at a time, but there are 17 light bulbs ready for use in my living room. If Kansas needs to build a new coal-fired plant to keep up with energy demands, you can blame me.

Anyway, behind my computer desk stands the new torchiere lamp, which bounces one hundred and fifty watts off the walls and the ceiling. It may be dark outside, but my living room shines like a summer day.

Because—it's better to buy another lamp than to curse the darkness.

December 2006

SEASONAL AMNESIA

Two weeks ago when the high temperature hit 70 degrees, forecasters warned us, in unison, that the good-weather party was about to end. So, when sleet clinked on the gutters of Emporia homes at 11 a.m. the next morning, it was not a big surprise.

We'd heard the forecast, and besides, we know from experience that sleet happens in November.

But our minds have been elsewhere since last winter—we've harvested wheat, planted iris, gone fishing. We've eaten funnel cakes, cotton candy, kettle corn. We've read novels, ridden horses, carved pumpkins.

This batch of icy weather didn't occur out of context, but still, it takes us a while to relearn the ways of winter. Most of us had forgotten how noisy sleet can be as it pellets our homes. It sounds like a spray of BBs against the siding. Especially after the warm week we had, it took us awhile to reconcile ourselves with ice, wind chill, and snow.

Kids spent that first afternoon looking for mittens, adults for ice scrapers. We had forgotten that out-of-control feeling we get when anti-lock brakes stutter. We wondered if those brakes would stop us before we slid into a Chevy Suburban.

The truth is, we don't recognize the value of traction until we discover a patch of polished ice that puts our tires in a tailspin.

So, we love the red-brown grit that the city tosses onto the streets. It keeps our vehicles from swimming on the roads and it eventually melts the ice and the snow. But then the splattered slush becomes white scabs on the sides of our cars. That deicer turns a vehicle into a salt lick.

Yes, we had forgotten so many things about winter. Memory

is only as long as a season.

We are being reintroduced to the whine of a tight and cold car engine. We feel that same tightness in our bodies as we hunch behind the steering wheel while the motor idles.

In the car, we are forced to remember the waiting period for warmth. I always ask politely: "Mr. Heat, please." But politeness matters not—hot, dry air is a long time coming. First Mr. Heat has to exhale all that cold air he's held in his lungs all night before he can get around to generating warmth.

Since last winter, we had forgotten the coldness of car seats, and that straight-jacket feeling of wearing both a bulky coat and a seatbelt.

When temperatures plunge into the teens so suddenly, we are surprised when freezing air crawls up the leg openings of our jeans.

And when cold air attacks, it is simply everywhere: invading your neckline, slipping under your coat at the waist, freezing the curve of your ears.

Everything vibrates at a lower level in wintertime and some things barely move. Fingers become red and less pliable. Your mind wills your fingers to bend, but thoughts are not as powerful as subfreezing temperatures.

During the season's first snowstorm, we are always shocked at the blinding whiteness of it all. We watch the tiny flakes fall as light as a wink and we wonder how many millions of snowflakes cover the lawn, how many scrunched up flakes it takes to build a snowman.

We had forgotten about puddles of water on the entry way floor and cold wet socks. We had forgotten about sore throats, Kleenex and chapped lips.

Those winter memories are returning as cold, hard facts.

Now the sun rises on frosty mornings, and I'll bet that most of us can't even recall the fierceness of the August sun, how the waistbands of our jeans can become heavy with sweat, or just how quickly chocolate melts inside a sun-baked car.

February 2006

THE WINTER THAT WASN'T

January showed up this year wearing shorts and a tank top. Although Kansas is the poster child for peculiar weather, temperatures last month were way out of sync with the calendar.

December, however, provided chilly temperatures and on one of those 20-degree days, Dave ordered a heavy coat from Cabela's. The package arrived the next week during that balmy after-Christmas weather.

"It's not cold enough to wear this," Dave said, pulling the coat from the box.

Dave is disappointed that he's been able to wear his new coat only once or twice. But me, I live with the motto, "Any day I don't have to wear a coat is a good day."

There were a lot of good days in January.

People were wary of the unusual warmth. Conversations often included remarks such as: "Can you believe this weather? We're gonna pay for this."

My friend Jay Price, who studies regional identity, perks his ears at comments such as these and once told me, "No one is more nervous than a Kansan during a stretch of good weather."

We had one of the warmest Januarys on record. I'm not complaining—for years I've railed against winter. My skin is thin and the cold hurts. Our house is drafty, the furnace inefficient. During normal winters, I wear three layers of long-sleeved shirts. A space heater keeps me company at my writing desk.

This past November though, I psyched myself up for winter. For the first time in my adult life, I was ready—really ready—to face the cold and the snow.

In a December column, I mentioned this quasi-conversion

experience and expressed appreciation for some of winter's qualities. After reading the column, my mother e-mailed me, concerned.

"What is wrong with you?" she asked.

But I actually didn't mind December's weather. When it did snow, twice, six inches each time, I delighted in the white stuff. And, as strange as it seemed, I did not feel the cold.

Then came January and its parade of 60-degree days. The *one* year I was happy to deal with winter—and the season fizzled. Maybe I scared it away.

As last month came to a close, I sent an e-mail to Steve Beylon, the morning meteorologist with KSNT-TV in Topeka. "Hey, what is up with this crazy weather?" I asked.

"The mild weather is due in part (key phrase there: 'in part') to La Niña," Beylon replied.

The cooling of Pacific waters near Ecuador and Peru starts a chain reaction that causes the jet stream to move northward. This weather pattern often "produces cool and damp weather in the Pacific Northwest and the moisture makes its way toward the Great Lakes. The Southern Plains often deals with drier and warmer than normal weather," he said.

Beylon mentioned that Topeka (and Emporia) had one of the warmest Januarys on record, second only to January 1933. Topeka's average temperatures for the month are normally in the mid- to upper 20s (average temperature = high + low, divided by 2.) However, the average this January was 41 degrees.

But we still have some winter ahead of us.

"Don't be surprised if your February heating bill is higher than January's heating bill," Beylon said during a broadcast.

Most winters, we are eager to be released from captivity. But no cabin fever this year. January knocked on the door and asked if we could come out and play.

Now that we have spent January taking walks, playing golf, waxing the car and working in the yard, will spring still have its magic? Sure it will.

And although I did well with the cold weather we've had, I'm sticking with my motto: Any day I don't have to wear a coat is a good day.

January 2010

FLINT HILLS IN WINTER

A red sunrise is the sign of things to come—and it's something I never care to see in the winter.

Dave and I hoped the snowfall would hold off until evening. The air temperature was 2 degrees when we headed to Salina on Jan. 2 for a holiday gathering that had been delayed because of the Christmas Eve blizzard.

Although I had shoveled about eight inches of Christmas snow from my walk and driveway here in Emporia, out in the country the blowing snow had hopscotched across the Flint Hills, sticking wherever the land grabbed it. Snow accumulated in deep drifts behind wind blocks, gathered in draws, and landed in trails on the hillsides where the grass had previously been pressed down by cattle hooves and pickup tires.

So the view was not of snowcapped hills, but rather of splotchy hills with tan grasses sticking up through white ground.

Because it was 2 degrees, I jokingly suggested, "Let's stop at the Tallgrass Preserve to see the bison." And Dave replied, "I'll bet they're all in the house today. Sleeping on the beds."

The car's CD player provided us with Beatles tunes. "Something (in the Way She Moves)" was playing, but a more appropriate song would have been "The Long and Winding Road" as we drove the Flint Hills Scenic Byway through the curves of wintry landscape.

Color was absent from the overcast sky and also from the earth. The spines of the trees were not their usual grayish color, but more of a black tone, leaving the valley farmland to look like a black-and-white photograph. The only color in sight came from the yellow stripes in the center of the highway.

Kansas was frozen and few people were venturing out.

Farmers and ranchers had to; they hauled hay to their livestock and chopped holes in ice so the animals could access water.

There's not only a harshness that comes with winter, but also a hardness. Water freezes on the tops of ponds and streams and stock tanks. The cold is so persistent that the soil becomes impenetrable. Nothing moves. Everything is locked in place.

Animals often face winter head-on. Cattle stood shoulder-to-shoulder. Hundreds of Canada geese gathered on a stubble field. That evening we would see deer "yarding up," feeding on fields in groups of 10 to 20.

Driving on a road in the hush of winter, we encountered very little traffic that morning. Winter creates a feeling that the world is on hold, as if we are traveling through a tunnel of time.

A small farm pond appeared to be frozen over, but who knows how thick the ice was. I suppose Alaskans or Minnesotans know how to calculate human weight versus time, temperature and thickness of ice, but I don't think I'll ever be the first one to step onto an icy pond.

Entering Council Grove from the south is the secret approach to town. Due to a series of hills, you can't see it from a distance, but you know Council Grove is coming because of the accumulation of billboards. I always wonder: Is it the crest of this hill or the next one that will reveal the city?

When popping over that final hill, you'll see houses resting in the valley and you slip into the quiet edge of town. "Where the past is always present," reads a welcome sign. At the Farmers and Drovers Bank at 9:04 that morning, the electronic sign announced that it was 0 degrees.

"Here Comes the Sun" came over the car's speakers. Wishful singing. The sky was gray-white above us and the gradient clouds became a darker blue around the north edge of the horizon. Snow clouds.

We drove on through the layers of winter: the cold, the crusty edges of snowplowed streets in Council Grove, the whiteness of salt on the highway. Snow would come that evening, after we had made the trip and returned safely home. It fell, several inches, adding another layer of winter to our lives.

Nature

May 2009

BACK TO NATURE

Nature is the original comeback kid.

If you clear underbrush, it returns. Burn off a pasture and that just makes it greener quicker. Neglect a building for a year or two and the weeds, woody vines and trees snuggle up against it. Nature's goal is to reclaim territory, to return the planet to wildness, to wilderness. The skin of the earth is continually trying to heal itself from human intervention.

I've seen dozens of abandoned silos in Kansas that have good-sized trees growing from the tops of them. It's nature's way of planting a flag, of proclaiming "mine."

Sixty mile-per-hour winds do their best to blow down wooden barns and once-white farmhouses. Rain and hail beat on them. Boards contract in the cold, expand in the heat. Nails loosen. The wood falls to the earth and decays, becoming one with the soil.

This is a normal process, matter changing form. It's that whole dust-to-dust thing that is part of life—but the concept of nature's reclamation of buildings has never been as obvious to me as it was on a recent visit to Neosho Falls.

Neosho Falls is a town of about 174 in Woodson County. (You'll find it just this side of Piqua.) There's no highway running into town, so the place doesn't get many passing-through visitors. To wind up here, you have to either be aiming for the town—or else be totally lost.

According to Daniel Fitzgerald in *Ghost Towns of Kansas,* Neosho Falls claimed county seat-hood in 1858. After a tug-of-war, in 1876 the Woodson County courthouse was awarded to Yates Center.

In 1879, it was reported that 40,000 people came to see President Rutherford B. Hayes when he stopped in Neosho Falls.

The town once had an active railroad and roundhouse. Oil was found here in 1937 and there was a spell of drilling.

"During the 1940s and 1950s several destructive fires and floods left the town in ruins," Fitzgerald wrote.

No, the flood of '51 did not go over well. Mother Nature is a pretty woman, but not always kind. People left the area.

I have a fondness for Neosho Falls. It's one of my favorite small towns in the state. I'm happy to report that there is again a gathering spot in town—the tavern has reopened as The Oasis.

During this recent visit to Neosho Falls, the vines caught my attention. Woodbine isn't as innocent as it appears to be.

On the main drag, several abandoned storefronts have been engulfed by these creeping vines. Trees are growing inside the buildings, limbs reaching out through window openings. Memorial Hall has been attacked by vines as well. In the summer this three-story red brick building looks like a leafy chia pet.

The woodbine grows unchecked. Climbing up the brick, the vines are opportunists, the foliage worms its way through mortar. Like fingers, the tendrils clutch onto bricks and pull them down one by one.

It's going to take some work to bring down the 1930s school building. This formidable structure has the appearance of an above-ground concrete bunker. But now without a roof or windows or doors, trees grow inside the auditorium, vines smother the walls.

Across from Riverside Park, where President Hayes made his appearance, is a structure that looks like an old Phillips 66 station. It's a small cottage-style building with a pointed roof. The stone cottage is swamped by trees and vines which camouflage it, making it practically invisible. Another building has been captured by nature—and is going down.

It's sad to see these old structures being swallowed whole. The brick, stone and wooden buildings have been placeholders of time, showing us that generations of Kansans lived here and thrived. Once upon a time.

I left town with mixed emotions. There's the feeling of loss—of history, of time, of the stories of people who once lived here. But nature offers a different version. She tells the story of wholeness, of overcoming, of starting anew.

October 2004

ON THE TALLGRASS PRAIRIE

If we all lived out in the country, there would be no countryside.

So some of us must live in towns and cities to keep the glorious Flint Hills free from the clutter of thousands of homes. In exchange for keeping the wide-open spaces wide open, we city dwellers like to visit the range occasionally.

The Tallgrass Prairie National Preserve provides a place and an opportunity for us to walk through the switch grass, the big and little bluestem, and to reach out and touch ironweed and blue sage.

On a recent Sunday afternoon, Dave and I drove to the Tallgrass Prairie, two miles north of Strong City on Kansas Highway 177.

We've visited the national preserve before but had toured only the house and the barn area. This time we wanted to wander through the hills and learn more about the prairie ecosystem.

So Dave and I hiked on the Southwind Nature Trail through six-foot-tall big bluestem and Indian grass, and we also took the 90-minute bus tour deep into the park. About 15 people were on the small bus that carried us on a path-like road through the pastures.

Originally from Indiana, Duane Baughman, who looked to be in his 30s, is a seasonal park ranger and frequently moves around to various national parks. Baughman drove the bus and was our interpretive tour guide. "This is the 13th place that I've lived and I've gotten to see a lot of this country. When I had the opportunity to come here, I was really excited," he said.

Baughman stopped the bus four or five times, giving us the chance to get out. He showed us a place that was, more than a century ago, a buffalo wallow. It's a spot where the ground is cracked and moisture is not too far below the surface.

Buffalo loosened the soil with their hooves to get to the water. They would stir up a batch of mud and then roll in it to help keep the insects off them.

Many springs flow on the 10,894 acres of the preserve.

"Some of the springs release seven to eight gallons of water per minute," Baughman said.

Along for the ride were two German-speaking families. One young family moved to the United States five years ago, and they live in Overland Park. The other family came from Germany for a visit.

"We wanted our friends to see this place," the Overland Park woman told me as her eyes moved across the expanse.

Meanwhile, two boys on the tour spotted a lizard running through the rocks.

Baughman showed us dried indigo plants. He pointed to small mounds of dirt that were "evidence of a pocket gopher."

Back in the bus, one woman asked, "What's that smell?"

"Fetid marigold," Baughman said. "It's growing in the center of the road."

"Everywhere I go," he said, "there's a smell that I remember from each place. Fetid marigold will be what I remember from Kansas."

It was an early autumn day. The air stood still. Above us were a dozen jet trails, most of them streaking from east to west, although two north-south contrails crossed over, drawing a tic-tac-toe game.

I always encounter a paradox on the empty prairie. Out here I may be isolated from the rest of the world, yet it is where I feel a complete connection with the universe.

Under the wide blue sky, in the middle of nearly 11,000 acres of grass and grasshoppers, monarchs and wildflowers, each one of us on that tour understood the absolute magnificence of the tallgrass prairie.

For more information, visit www.nps.gov/tapr.

October 2007

OUR TROPICAL PAST

What's more fun than a box of rocks?

I'll tell you: it's seeing rocks in their natural environment out in the Flint Hills.

These stones come with stories. Now, the rocks don't talk to me, but apparently they do have a lot to say to geologists.

It took a long time to get Kansas looking the way she does.

Oceans came and oceans went and the seas that covered Kansas left behind layers of stone. Limestone, which underlies much of the Flint Hills, was created from the skeletons of marine organisms. We're talking a lot of time here. It was about 300 million years ago that the Permian Period seas floated over the land that is now Kansas.

More recently, on Sept. 22, Rex Buchanan and Bob Sawin of the Kansas Geological Survey led about 30 people on a geological hike at the Tallgrass Prairie National Preserve near Strong City.

Rex Buchanan is associate director for public outreach and Bob Sawin is a research associate for the geology extension. The KGS is located at the University of Kansas in Lawrence. These men are familiar with the Tallgrass Preserve. They've both spent time here, walking the land to track down springs on the property.

On the geology hike, our first stop was at the 1881 farmhouse to examine Cottonwood limestone in the structure. Embedded in the stone are fusulinids: wheat-shaped fossils that were one-celled organisms.

Used as a diagnostic fossil, these fusulinids help date and identify stones. Cottonwood limestone is named after Cottonwood Falls. The names for geologic units are derived from the location where they are discovered.

There are many types of limestone. While walking in the Flint Hills, you may stumble across white stones with holes in them.

"The holes are one of the characteristics of Eiss limestone," Sawin said. "A few years ago, we inventoried all the springs. Eiss had a lot of springs associated with it. The holes not only stored water but allowed it to move through."

A core sample showed that the Eiss limestone contained gypsum, "which is real soluble," Sawin said. "That explains the holes."

As you look across the Flint Hills landscape, you can see a step-like aspect, which is due to alternating layers of shale and limestone.

"The limestone is more resistant to weathering (than the shale)," Sawin said.

Layered in with the limestone is chert (also called flint), which is even harder than the limestone.

"Chert has a very characteristic fracture pattern," Buchanan told us. It has sharp-edged breaks; that's why Native Americans used the stone for arrowheads.

In a road-cut along K-177, Buchanan pointed out brachiopod fossils in the limestone.

"You very seldom see these (fossils) whole," he said. The high-energy environment of waves crashing upon a seashore tends to break up would-be fossils. "It's a very tough environment for that kind of preservation."

Buchanan mentioned transgression and regression of the seas. A number of oceans came and went, creating those layers of shale, limestone and chert. The waters would have been shallow and warm.

"We're looking at a record of what the climate was like here," Buchanan said. "If you want to know what Kansas looked like 300 million years ago, go to the Caribbean," he said.

So, in its past life, Kansas was like the Caribbean? Sigh. I was born 300 million years too late.

Kansas has a long and rocky history, but our past is far from dull and dry. Once upon a time, Kansas was warm and wet and splashy.

June 2007

HUNTING THE KANSAS PLAYA

Dave and I recently found ourselves on a new Kansas adventure: playa hunting.

It was new to me, anyway. I'd never even heard of playas. But apparently there are about 2,000 of them on the High Plains of Kansas.

North of Garden City on a windy May morning, Jim and Susie Aber introduced Dave and me to these wetlands. The Abers are both geologists and teach at Emporia State University.

Jim explained that a playa is "a depression that has water on an ephemeral basis."

Susie added that it's an enclosed basin with no inlet or outlet—kind of like a natural pothole in the land.

"It's a characteristic of semi-arid landscapes," Jim said.

Western Kansas normally gets less than 20 inches of annual precipitation. So most years, maybe 9 out of 10, the playas are dry. But this has been an unusually wet winter and spring out there; playas are full.

The Abers took advantage of this wet year. To document and study the playas, they photographed them from the air with a kite.

Hang out with scientists and you're likely to learn something. That day, not only did Dave and I learn about playas, but we also got to see kite aerial photography in action.

Using a 300-pound-test line, the Abers launched a kite. They have ordinary digital cameras, "oodles of kites" and a remote control that allows them to snap aerial photos from the ground.

"This is high-tech stuff," Susie joked. "We're using dog leashes," she laughed, pointing to the blue and pink leashes that tethered the kite reel to their truck. The wooden kite reel is a couple of feet wide and looks like something you might use for deep-sea fishing.

"It's not fancy equipment," Susie said, "but we've taken some fantastic pictures."

One of their aerial photos of an Estonian bog won first place in a contest sponsored by the American Association for Advancement of Science.

"Except for the rig for the camera, everything is off the shelf," Jim said.

On the day we were with them, sustained winds blew at 19–22 mph, which is about the maximum speed at which they'll fly a camera. Optimal speeds are 7–10 mph.

"We fly a long tail to increase the stability of the kite," Jim said.

They send their kites up to 500 feet. Higher than that, they'd need to file a flight plan with an airport. Jim looked through binoculars to see the antenna on the camera rig. From this he could determine the angle and direction of the camera lens. The kite flew about 450 feet above the ground.

"Left. Take. Left. Take," Jim said, directing Susie how to maneuver the camera using the remote control.

"You never know what you're getting until the camera is back on the ground," Susie said. "The fun thing about the kite is that it's up high enough up to see the big picture, but low enough to see the detail."

The Abers have been sending cameras up kite strings since 1996. They've used kite aerial photography to study land patterns not only in the United States, but also in Poland, Norway, Estonia, Denmark and Slovakia.

They keep returning to Cheyenne Bottoms in Barton County, one of their long-term projects.

"Cheyenne Bottoms is kind of a giant playa," Jim said. "Last year it was mostly dry; this year it's flooded."

What's important to them as earth scientists, Susie said, is "repeated imagery of the same site to show how it changes over time."

"The pulsing of the landscape is fascinating to watch."

To view aerial photos taken by the Abers, check their website: www.geospectra.net.

July 2008

ROCK CITY, USA

Years ago, when I moved to Emporia, one friend would ask me from time to time, "Aren't you from Rock City?"

"No," I'd say, "Pawnee Rock. I'm from Pawnee Rock."

After hearing the place mentioned so often, I decided that one day I would visit this fabled Rock City. The day had finally arrived. Rock City, here we come.

On the Fourth of July, Dave and I were in the neighborhood (Salina), so we drove north about 20 miles to see the site. This Registered Natural Landmark is a few miles southwest of Minneapolis (pop. 2,015), the county seat of Ottawa County.

Rock City is just a small patch of land—they describe it as the size of two football fields—with about 200 sphere-shaped boulders scattered on the ground.

To me, it looked like teams of giants had been called away unexpectedly and left their croquet balls on the pasture. Some of the round boulders are 3–4 feet high, some 10–12 feet. Rock City is simply a bunch of sandstone rocks grouped together, sort of lined up, resting on the grassy sea.

What are these rocks and how did they get there?

I checked with Jim Aber, professor of geology at Emporia State University, who told me:

"The large spherical structures at Rock City are examples of concretions, which are common in the Dakota formation. This is a Cretaceous formation that is widespread in the Great Plains—from Pawnee Rock to Rock City to the Black Hills.

"In places, the sandstone was cemented around organic nuclei," Aber said. "Where the softer, uncemented rock weathers away, the harder cemented concretions become exposed at the surface, as at Rock City, Mushroom Rock State Park and many other localities."

These sandstone rocks are part of our state's surf-to-turf history. Kansas has a number of geological surprises and Rock City is one of them.

In the gift shop I visited with Sylvia Skanks, who has worked there for 10 years, providing information about Rock City and the area. The shop sells T-shirts and ball caps as well as regional cookbooks and crafts by local residents.

She likes to keep records and told me that in May and June, 1,364 visitors had stopped by Rock City. So far in 2008, tourists had come from 43 states, as well as from Germany, Canada, Colombia and Kyrgyzstan.

Sylvia invited us to wander around and take photos. "And if you want a picture of you two taken together I'll come out and do that," she offered.

She enjoys her job out there in the country and often takes a chair outside. "I like nature," she said. "I watch the birds. A mamma bird had her babies down on the ground awhile ago."

The air was still that morning at Rock City, but it wasn't quiet. Off in the distance, combines hummed through the wheat fields. Closer, I heard the call of a bobwhite. White butterflies flickered over the purple poppy mallow. Lizards zipped around on the stones, unwilling to pose for photographs.

In the stillness of the morning I tried to imagine what the settlers must have thought in the 1800s when they discovered the boulders. As they trekked across the prairie, these peculiar spheres must have made them tilt their heads and mutter, "Huh?"

Rock City isn't a flashy tourist attraction. There are no roller coasters here, and there's no indoor plumbing, but visitors are likely to be intrigued and amazed when pondering these boulders and their presence on the open prairie.

In Kansas, we're about as far away from the sea coasts as anyone in the United States can be.

We are far away not only in distance but also in time. Still, in this landlocked state, we can always find evidence of our oceanic past.

October 2009

IN DENIAL

It was akin to being told I was adopted. I learned one little bit of information and was forced to rethink my entire childhood.

You see, I was raised on level land. From Pawnee Rock, we'd drive 8 miles west to Larned or 12 miles east to Great Bend, and all around me the horizon was one straight-as-a-ruler flat line.

Conclusion: I was a child of the plains.

The image of my homeland, the picture that is etched into my brain, is from the top of Pawnee Rock State Historic Site. Known locally as the Rock, that outcropping of Dakota sandstone was used in the 1800s as a lookout point along the Santa Fe Trail—and it was from that high vantage point that I memorized the wide view of the Arkansas River Valley.

Standing on the Rock on a haze-free day, I'd spot the Burdett water tower about 20 miles to the west; closer to me were the towers in Rozel and Larned.

About a mile and a half south of the Rock was a line of trees marking the Arkansas River. To the southeast, I could spot the grain elevators in Radium and Seward.

Flat land. Flaaaaat land. As in no hills to block the view.

But then this past summer, Jim and Susie Aber, friends of the geological variety, suggested in their book, which details the Kansas physiographic regions, that my hometown rides the border of the Smoky Hills.

Oh, no, no, no, no, no. This cannot be right. There were no hills around us.

While reading "Kansas Physiographic Regions: Bird's-eye Views," my eyes stopped, stunned, on page 37. There, the Abers include in the Smoky Hills region the rock formation known as Pawnee Rock.

Apparently, a thin stripe of the Smoky Hills province slides through Barton, Pawnee and Hodgeman counties. The town of Pawnee Rock teeters on the boundary line between two regions: the Arkansas River Valley and the Smoky Hills.

The Rock's Dakota sandstone helps define it as part of the Smoky Hills. Similar sandstone is found at Coronado Heights near Lindsborg, Mushroom Rock State Park in Ellsworth County and Rock City near Minneapolis.

The river valley part of my childhood landscape was a given, but it just never would have occurred to me that the Rock was part of the Smoky Hills—as in hills.

Sure there are hills in Kansas, but not where I grew up . . . or were there?

Well, of course, we had that one obvious hill, Pawnee Rock State Park. It's definitely a hill, although I always thought of it as more of a freak of nature than a legitimate hill.

And let's see, from the Rock, there's not really a view to the north. Trees aside, you can't look 20 miles northward like you can in the other directions. Instead of the long vista, the land just kind of ends. OK, that indicates soft rolling hills—which, I'll admit now, do exist north of town.

For it was on those rolling hills that my grandfather gave us a roller coaster simulation, that sensation of leaving one's stomach behind.

In the pre-seatbelt era, my brother and cousins and I would already be bouncing in the backseat of Grandpa's Chevy Impala. On those hills near his farm, we'd shout, "Make us lose our stomachs, Grandpa!" He would chuckle and speed up, cresting the hills and flying over them.

So the hills were steep enough for that.

Yet if anyone had asked me during my youth about topography, I'd have said, no, no hills, the land is flat.

Since the geologists tell me my hometown is on the edge of the Smoky Hills, well, I'll have to go along with it. Because, after all, it is from the top of a hill that I have my treasured view of the flat land.

Maybe I just can't see the hills for the plains.

April 2010

CHEYENNE BOTTOMS

I've probably driven through Cheyenne Bottoms a couple of dozen times in my life. This wetlands area is in Barton County, about 20 miles from my childhood home. But I'm not an outdoorsman or a biologist, and, to be honest, my bird identification skills are a little weak, so I don't suppose that I ever quite "got" Cheyenne Bottoms.

Cheyenne Bottoms is a 64-square-mile wetlands basin and has been called "the most important migration point for shorebirds in North America." It is estimated that 45 percent of North American shorebirds stop at Cheyenne Bottoms during spring migration to rest and refuel.

Recently, while in Great Bend, Dave and I took my dad and stepmother on a drive to this wetlands area. It was late March, the air was full of wind and rain and it was in the mid-40s, not a pleasant day to be outside. So it seemed like a perfect opportunity to tour the Kansas Wetlands Education Center. The center, located at the edge of the bottoms along Kansas Highway 156 between Claflin and Great Bend, opened about a year ago and is a branch of Fort Hays State University's Sternberg Museum of Natural History.

Jason Black, a graduate student from FHSU, was working at the center that day. Through the building's viewing window, he pointed out a blue-winged teal and a couple of magnificent white and black birds—American avocets. The avocets have long legs and long, upturned bills.

"Avocets are readily identifiable, and they are beautiful in flight," Black said, adding that the avocet is on the center's logo. So, yay, I can now identify a shorebird.

The Kansas Wetlands Education Center provides an impressive introduction to Cheyenne Bottoms. The value and benefits of wetlands are explained and a timeline tells about changes to Cheyenne Bottoms over the years.

The center has samples of bird eggs and nests and general information, including this fascinating fact: "At night, the birds navigate using the stars and earth's magnetic field. By sensing the magnetic fields, birds detect north and orient their direction of flight to the patterns of stars."

Isn't that incredible?

Cheyenne Bottoms is along the Wetlands and Wildlife National Scenic Byway, which is one of the nine state byways in Kansas. This particular byway has a helpful (and free) traveling brochure and a CD to listen to as you drive the 77-mile route. Beginning in Hoisington, the byway tours Cheyenne Bottoms and then heads south into Stafford County and through the Quivira National Wildlife Refuge.

As we puttered along the causeways, watching ducks bob on the waves, seeing a flock take off in massive flight, we listened to the CD and heard local experts and residents speak about migrating birds, bloodworms, conservation, and the splendor of Cheyenne Bottoms.

Carl Grover, a hunter, told about sitting in the cattails with his son one day when a muskrat swam up and groomed itself, just three feet away. "That made the day," Grover said. "It didn't matter if we didn't shoot a duck, didn't matter if we didn't see a duck. We were in the marsh; we experienced what goes on out there."

Bob Matthews, chief of information and education with the Kansas Department of Wildlife and Parks, put into words what I was experiencing that day. "Until you get to know somebody," he said, "they're just a stranger. But once you get to know them, you find out all these things about them that are intriguing and fascinating, and things that you would never have known otherwise without personal interaction with that person.

"It's sorta like that when you go out on the marsh . . . and you encounter an individual bird or an individual critter and maybe you've seen a picture of it before but have never seen it in person . . . and all of the sudden you have a little more common ground there with that critter, a little more interest, a little more appreciation for it, and a little more commitment to it as well."

Yes, absolutely. I gained some knowledge of the wetlands, and I can now identify the American avocet and several other winged creatures. By discovering that birds use stars and magnetic fields to navigate, by learning just how much these migrating birds depend on Cheyenne Bottoms for their survival, I get it. I do have more interest, more appreciation, and more commitment to the wetlands and to Cheyenne Bottoms.

For more information, visit www.kansaswetlandsandwildlifescenicbyway.com.

July 2007

THE MOUNTAINS

They had been holding out on me.

"You mean this was here all the time?" I asked my parents as our car, unaccustomed to high altitude, sputtered up a Rocky Mountain highway west of Denver.

Photographs of mountains had not prepared an 11-year-old Kansas kid for this much dirt, so many rocks, millions of trees. It looked as if Mom's pinking shears had snipped the landscape. Gray and white mountaintops were like jagged teeth cutting into the postcard-blue sky.

Raised on two-dimensional land, I knew only length and width until Colorado—macho, rugged and handsome—elevated me into the world of 3-D. Childhood trips to visit my grandparents in the Arkansas hills had taught me nothing about mountains.

In the early 1970s, on our first real family vacation, the car crept around hairpin curves on Trail Ridge Road in Rocky Mountain National Park. The Rockies filled the windshield. Colorado had more earth than sky. The way I figured, a person could scrape together all the dirt in Kansas and only build about four mountains, maybe five.

In Colorado, our '65 Dodge didn't hover over the land like it did on the prairie. The car ascended peaks and then dove into canyons. Surrounded by dirt walls, we seemed to be submerged in the earth.

Dad stopped at every scenic overlook for us to gawk and to take photographs and by the time we got above the timberline, I was smitten with Colorado. Who wouldn't be? The air, thin and tingly, could make the dead dance a jig.

It was that dry air that felt so good. The shortage of oxygen made me inhale deeply, taking in the clean smell of pine.

We had outclimbed the trees and from 12,000 feet, I saw a kingdom of mountaintops in every direction, the peaks bright with snow. It was summertime, probably July, and at one stop, my brother and I ran up the mountainside to see who could shape the first snowball. Mom cautioned us to watch our step. She was looking out for the delicate alpine flowers, which had a short-enough lifespan without us trampling them.

Using binoculars at the visitors center, we spotted bighorn sheep grazing on a mountainside. In the gift store, I bought a copper bracelet, something that would help me remember this perfect place. I was swallowed up by Colorado, so much that I could hardly stand it. I had fallen in love with this aggressive landscape, which was yang to Kansas' yin.

One night, our family rented a cabin along one of a million fast-moving streams in the state. Late that afternoon, I sat alone on the edge of the forest and listened as the white water bounced over rocks, running as fast as it could in search of an ocean.

I absorbed the surroundings, hoping to remember everything—the sharp-edged boulders, the smooth river rocks, the smell of spruce—and I vowed that someday, somehow, I would return to Colorado.

Later, eastbound through the foothills, I twisted in the backseat, wanting to lasso the Rockies and drag them back to Kansas. Now that I'd seen them, breathed them, marked them on my soul, could I live without mountains?

Yeah, I could. After a few days, the flat land reclaimed me. I lost the crushed-ice taste of thin mountain air, could no longer smell the fragrance of freshly torn pine needles, forgot about the smooth water of lakes high in the mountains.

However, I've made good on my childhood promise; I've returned to Colorado about 10 times, most recently this past spring. The prairie is long and lean and beautiful, but sometimes, you just have to climb a mountain.

Looking Back

January 2004

ECHOES OF PAWNEE ROCK

My hometown doesn't have much, but it does have the Rock, an unexpected outcropping of Dakota sandstone rising above the otherwise flat Arkansas River Valley.

"Pawnee Rock springs like a huge wart from the carpeted green of the prairie" is how writer Matt Field described it in an 1840 *New Orleans Picayune* newspaper article.

As youngsters, my friends and I took advantage of Pawnee Rock State Park, located on the town's north edge.

With corduroys tucked into rubber boots, we dragged our sleds up that hill and sped down the snowy white roadway or slipped between trees on the Rock's north side.

On summer days, the Rock was always a good destination for a bicycle ride. My friends and I climbed around on the rocks; sometimes we hunted lizards. We talked with the ever-present tourists who had pulled off U.S. Highway 56, and we looked for Kit Carson's name, which was supposedly carved in the stone.

On the Rock's flat top is a monument and a pavilion. The stone-and-concrete pavilion rises about 20 feet above the ground. A spiral staircase leads to its upper level. From there you have a wide-open view of the plains.

Recently, Emporian Gwen Zimmerman stopped by *The Gazette* office and dropped off a copy of a page from *Echoes of Pawnee Rock.* It was an article written by William Allen White, titled "Monuments and Things."

"The story that the great rock symbolizes, as it is told and retold, cannot but make a deep impression on the life of this community," White wrote.

The small book, *Echoes of Pawnee Rock,* published in 1908, raised funds for the Women's Kansas Day Club. The club's purpose was to preserve historic places in the state. Because a large portion of the sandstone had already been quarried (probably including the stone with Kit Carson's name), the club stepped in to save the site from further destruction.

The Pawnee Rock community and the Women's Kansas Day Club raised enough money to purchase the five acres and create Pawnee Rock State Park. A stone monument was dedicated in 1912 with a reported 8,000 people in attendance.

Easily seen from a distance, Pawnee Rock was a famous landmark along the Santa Fe Trail.

"We were part of an afternoon, and the greater part of the next day traveling with Pawnee Rock in sight before us," Matt Field noted in his newspaper article.

And the Rock served as a valuable lookout point. Anyone on top of the Rock had the upper hand. Gazing over the otherwise level and treeless landscape, one could see whatever approached: elk, buffalo, wagon trains, Indians or soldiers.

In the early to mid-1800s, this lookout point was the site of deadly combat. Intertribal skirmishes happened here, as did as many battles between white men and Indians.

In another article in *Echoes of Pawnee Rock,* Margaret Perkins quoted the writing of a Barton County pioneer: "As for bloody battles fought around this old Rock, I should judge they were numerous; for when I came here many graves were discernible."

He continued, "Well I remember the fall and winter of 1872 when a party of St. Louis bone pickers camped under the shelter of Pawnee Rock. Those sixteen cars, packed for shipment by my brother and me, did not contain buffalo bones only. Just how many human skeletons we packed, I cannot now say, but fully ten skulls went to St. Louis."

I grew up in Pawnee Rock aware of the vague but deep history of the place.

We'll never know all the details of its history. But up on the Rock, standing in a warm south breeze, one can sometimes feel the presence of the many people who passed through and of the many people who died here.

For more on Pawnee Rock, past and present, visit PawneeRock.org.

May 2004

A RIDE INTO HISTORY

"I am Amelia Earhart. It is April 14, 1937."

As Ann Birney of Admire took the stage at the Kansas Sampler Festival in Newton recently, she also took the audience into the world of Amelia Earhart.

When she wears the leather flight jacket, a white scarf tied loosely around her neck and khaki-colored vintage trousers, Birney becomes the famous pilot. Birney's face is freckled, her short brown hair loose and curly. She has the enthusiasm one would expect of the tomboyish Amelia.

"No one pays me to fly planes; they pay me to talk about them and to write about them," Birney said, acting the role of Earhart.

"Today I thought I would be halfway around the world," she said, and described the wreck of her plane as it took off from Hawaii on her first around-the-world attempt.

"We had to take the Electra back to the Lockheed plant on a boat. And there's nothing a plane hates worse than being taken someplace by boat."

"Everyone asks me about my first flight. My first flight was in Atchison," she said.

One Christmas, Amelia's father gave her a sled. Amelia and her sister Pidge rubbed a candle on its metal runners to make it go fast. They took the sled up a steep hill in Atchison.

"The wind was blowing through my hair," she said of the ride. Near the bottom of the hill, however, was a wagon and horse.

"I let out a yell," she said. But the driver's hat was pulled over his ears and the horse wore blinders.

"I steered that sled the best that I could and I went ZING—through the legs of the horse," she said, swooping her body.

"So I like to say that was my first flight . . . , but of course that had nothing to do with airplanes."

Ann Birney and Joyce Thierer operate Ride into History (www.rideintohistory.com) from a farm near Admire. Thierer's signature character is Calamity Jane. Both women give professional performances around the country and also teach others how to research and develop first-person narratives.

"Dr. Birney is one of the matriarchs of Kansas historical performers. I think everyone who has appeared on this stage has taken workshops from Ride into History," the announcer had said as he introduced her.

Before her on-stage appearance, I visited with Birney.

"What do you think happened to Amelia?" I asked.

"I have to take off my jacket to answer that," she said, putting it aside and picking up an old globe.

"This is Howland Island," Birney said, pointing to the area where she believes Earhart's plane ran out of fuel and crashed into the ocean.

"What do you most want for people to get out of your performances?" I asked.

"One of the things I say in the performance, something Amelia said, 'A plane does not care who you are as long as you can fly it.' And that this also applies to life—that you should try whatever it is you want to do and not let other people determine what risks you will take to get there."

About a dozen historical performers appeared at the festival.

Nolan Sump of Salina portrayed a German immigrant settler in 1880. After his performance, he talked about the importance of knowing our agricultural history.

"We have to remember where we come from. We're losing the family farms," he said.

There were six stages on the festival grounds. Musicians and jugglers, poets, dancers and clowns entertained. I saw the depth and passion of Kansans, entertainers who had acknowledged their talents and pursued their dreams.

As Amelia Earhart said, "A plane does not care who you are as long as you can fly it."

October 2007

THE VICTORY LAP

On April 27, 1945, Emporia held a carnival in the Civic Auditorium to sell war bonds. The event raised $20,122. Lyon County residents were financing a B-29 Superfortress for World War II.

At the carnival, the public learned the B-29 was to be named the "William Allen White" after the late editor of *The Emporia Gazette*. The 11-man crew assigned to this Wichita-built plane came to Kansas to take possession of the aircraft, and they came to Emporia to encourage the sale of war bonds.

Emporia honored the crew at the Civic Auditorium that evening. These young men in their twenties also paid a visit to the White home, where they met White's widow, Sallie.

Off to war they went. Two separate crews flew this particular bomber in daring missions over Japan, and the B-29 kept them safe.

Because these airmen had visited Emporia on their way to war, it makes me wonder what memories of our town they carried with them to Tinian Island in 1945. Each time they boarded the B-29 and saw the name William Allen White painted on that silver plane, did they feel the support of the Emporia people?

Roger Heineken of the William Allen White Community Partnership had been in contact with some of the crew via e-mail. When the men learned they would be in Wichita for a reunion of their bombing group, they said they wanted to revisit Emporia.

On Sept. 29, 2007, 62 years after their first trip here, three of the 11 crew members returned to Emporia's Civic Auditorium, and they also revisited White's home, now a state historic site.

Those three veterans were Jim Meeks of Valrico, Florida, the radio operator on the aircraft; Karl Samuels, from Slidell,

Louisiana, central fire control gunner; and Gin Wong of Los Angeles, the radar bombardier/navigator.

The day officially belonged to these vets. The mayor signed a proclamation designating Sept. 29 "'William Allen White' Crew and the City of Emporia Reunion Day."

Their return coincided with another event—the William Allen White Children's Book Awards. So, once again, these gentlemen appeared at the Civic Auditorium. They were given a standing ovation by hundreds of children at the book awards ceremony.

The men, now in their eighties, took a tour of the White house. The last time they stood in White's second-floor study, they were young men.

After the tour, the crewmen sat on the porch and related some of their war experiences. They talked about near-misses that occurred because the airspace over the western Pacific was often crowded with planes. They told about 16- and 17-hour missions and having no place to refuel.

The crew took shortcuts to return from Japan to Tinian Island. "Any way to get home," Wong said.

"We were only supposed to be flying fast enough to be staying in the air," Meeks added.

"One time we landed and two engines cut out," Samuels said. "Taxiing in on the runway, we ran out of gas."

On this recent September Saturday, history came home; three World War II veterans returned to Emporia for a victory lap. As they toured the White house, I could imagine them as the young men they were on their first visit. But this time, instead of talking with Sallie White, they met her great-grandson, Chris White Walker, and his daughters, Grace and Hattie. While watching the interactions of the crewmen with the latest of the White generations, I realized that these veterans touched two ends of history, the past and the present.

And the future. For they met the two sparkling girls, Grace and Hattie, who, in their early years of childhood, have yet to learn how years can proceed both quickly and slowly, and who have yet to understand the greatness of those men who were brave enough to save the world.

October 2004

THAT LONESOME WHISTLE

Each night before falling asleep, I listen for one last train. With ears perked like a cat, I wait. Will the next train come from the west or the east?

Soon, I hear a roar rise from the west.

As the nighttime locomotive chugs in from Strong City, I picture that long-tailed train slicing through the countryside, the Cyclops headlight eyeing its way in the dark. Louder and louder the rhythm grows, like a sewing machine running full speed. As this rolling crescendo hits town, the train bursts into song.

The train blares with the brassiness of a trumpet as it approaches each crossing.

Most of the whistles have a similar pitch and tone, yet they are played differently. Each locomotive engineer blows the whistle in his own style. A few of the engineers blast aggressively, laying on the horn. With other trains, I hear gentle, flutelike notes, with a soft attack and easy release.

I suppose if my house stood within a few blocks of the railroad tracks, the sound of trains might be a racket instead of a pleasant voice in the distance. If I lived nearby, the soft rhythmic rumble that I hear now could be a window rattler instead of a lullaby. The screaming whistles might jump me out of sleepiness instead of tucking me in with a sweet "goodnight."

I spent some time recently at Fremont Park at Fourth and Union streets. There I watched some of the pumpkin-colored Burlington Northern Santa Fe locomotives pull through town.

From 40 feet away, the train whistles are deafening. Locomotives shout their warning down the line, parting a sea of traffic.

Clattering flatbeds and boxcars chase after the yowling

locomotive. Some of the connections grind and squeal like automobile brakes. A few train wheels have rough spots or something that makes them run with a limp.

At Fremont Part, a black Santa Fe steam locomotive and a red caboose are on display. But they are for viewing only, surrounded by a chain-link fence. On the ground facing the railroad tracks, spelled out in large concrete letters, is the word "Emporia." A raised border surrounds the chipped letters.

I had no idea this town sign existed, although it's obvious it was created decades ago for the benefit of railroaders and passengers.

Perhaps flowers once grew among the concrete letters. I could picture a woman riding a passenger train through town, say in the 1940s, and noticing this Emporia sign blooming in the park.

For many of us, trains grabbed our imaginations when we were young.

Before my friends and I had driver's licenses and were able to leave that small town on our own, we sat at the depot in Pawnee Rock, our legs swinging from the loading dock as we waited for a train to pass through.

Trains came and went. We didn't; we were stuck. What was down those shiny tracks, we didn't know, but we wanted to find out.

Not many trains passed through Pawnee Rock, so it was a big deal when my friends and I saw that jittery light coming toward us. As the freight train approached, we stood up and waved frantically as if we could make it stop and whisk us away.

The engineer waved back and gave the whistle an extra toot before the locomotive and its boxcars disappeared into the world, leaving us behind.

Years later, trains still hold that dream of escape, the expectation of adventure. At bedtime, as a rumble lulls me to sleep, my thoughts leap aboard the passing train and ride it deep into the night.

January 2010

LEFT BEHIND

I'm thrilled when I see a small but thriving Kansas community, one with occupied storefronts, a café, a colorful downtown and maybe a few pieces of public art.

Yes, indeed, I love it when a town lives up to its potential.

And yet, I'm also drawn to the not-quite-making-it towns, the places with crumbling buildings, with brick and stone structures that have no roofs, the towns with an imploding general store whose wooden exterior walls haven't seen paint since the Eisenhower administration.

While I appreciate well-maintained buildings, I'm really fascinated by these neglected ones because the scene is often as the owner left it. There's an incomplete but authentic history here, and stories from the old days seem to linger in the air.

I'm not sure why I'm drawn to these buildings—maybe I'm trying to connect with lost parts of myself that I've abandoned over time. Or maybe these places just feel so familiar because during my childhood years, my hometown produced more and more empty structures.

As youngsters, my friends and I crawled around in a two-story brick building that once housed the *Pawnee Rock Herald.* We explored an old cabin that was moved into town. Down by the river, we toured the round barn—it still smelled like horses—and we investigated the adjacent unlocked farmhouse. As I looked at the wallpaper, the curtains, the dinette table, I wondered who the people were who had lived there and wondered why they had left.

While visiting small towns, I photograph these decaying structures because someday these buildings will go. They will fall down, blow down, burn down, and I want to document as many as I can before they vanish, before these particular architectural forms disappear from the landscape.

Peering into old buildings, you may be able to spot a few remaining items: a 1974 calendar on the wall, the Rainbo Bread push bar on the grocery store door, a sticker on the old post office window in which Mr. ZIP says, "Use ZIP code, the last word in mail address."

These buildings have a well-worn character, they retain the energy of the personalities who lived or worked in them. The tin ceilings, the dust-covered display cases, the rusted tools are the keepers of firsthand history. Stories are held here in escrow.

As a person sheds a storefront, they may leave pieces of their work days behind, a broken chair, a bench with saw marks, handwritten receipts. The shades of paint on the walls give a sense of the aesthetics of the 1940s or 1950s, as do the style of light fixtures and the woodwork, which may be either rustic or well crafted.

The barber shop door may have a hasp and padlock on it, but the windows have been gone for decades, the roof for a dozen years.

Standing on shards of broken glass beside the faded barber's pole, you might be able to feel the presence of the man with the clippers—and even imagine the chatter in his shop, the gossip passed on during the course of a day.

At these downtown businesses, I try to picture what kind of people the owners were. Did they enjoy their work? Did their children skip around in the aisles of the dry goods store while the shopkeeper helped a customer with her selection of fabric or buttons or thread?

And I'm curious about those customers of years gone by, I wonder what kind of concerns they had on a January morning a hundred years ago, while outside the breath of their horses rose like smoke in the wintry air.

While some people may consider these dilapidated places to be eyesores and even though the town may be enhanced—and made safer—by their removal, I appreciate the structures for the cultural history they offer.

Building styles and materials change. Small town businesses now often construct metal buildings which don't seem as permanent or as inviting as the old ones made of wood and brick and stone. Classic wooden barns are being replaced by metal barns and sheds.

Architecture from the early 1900s is a part of our collective history. Many of these buildings are collapsing, yet surely the stories of our ancestors hang from the corners like cobwebs. Next time you come across an abandoned building, take a moment to lean against the outside wall and have a listen.

January 2010

IKE AND THE INTERSTATES

In the year 2110 when Kansans fly around in their Jetson-like space cars, the occupants will probably spot parallel mounds of raised earth running for miles across the state.

"What are those lines on the ground, Mommy? Were they made by aliens?"

"No, honey, that's all that remains of the Kansas Turnpike," the mother will say. "A hundred years ago, people drove their cars from Emporia to Topeka. I read about it in my great-grandmother's electronic journal."

"They used ground transportation to travel 50 miles? Weird."

Oh, who knows what the world will be like in a hundred years? I sure don't, but like everything else, transportation modes change. Someday our highway system may not exist.

After all, the dusty and dangerous Santa Fe Trail is history, train travel has diminished and one of the most famed highways of all time, Route 66, is now in bits and pieces.

But for the present, interstate highways are an easy way to zoom across the state or the country. Along them, you may see the occasional roadside sign, white on blue, with a circle of five stars (for the five-star general) above the text "Eisenhower Interstate System."

Dwight D. Eisenhower's vision for interstate highways began with his participation in a two-month-long military caravan from Washington, D.C., to San Francisco in 1919. "Roads varied from average to non-existent," he said.

In his book, *At Ease: Stories I Tell to Friends,* Eisenhower said the military convoy was plagued with equipment breakdowns, but also roads and bridges were found lacking. "In some places, the heavy trucks broke through the surface of the road and we had to tow them out one by one. . . . Some days when we had counted on 60 or 70 or 100 miles, we would do three or four," he wrote.

The trip offered the future general and president a somber outlook for national security. If the United States needed to move equipment across the country quickly, we'd be in trouble, he thought.

Then, during World War II, General Eisenhower came across the autobahn in Germany. "The old convoy had started me thinking about good, two-lane highways, but Germany had made me see the wisdom of broader ribbons across the land," he said.

After Eisenhower became president, he pushed for a new highway system. "When we finally secured the necessary congressional approval, we started the 41,000 miles of super highways that are already proving their worth," he wrote in 1967.

I was born during the Eisenhower presidency. Growing up, I didn't live anywhere near an interstate, so I don't remember the construction period. But perhaps some of you recall those days when land was condemned and surveyed and the roads were built.

Ike's vision gave us our four-lane superhighways with their medians and limited access, overpasses, cloverleaf interchanges—and a whole new way of driving.

There are numerous firsts recorded with the construction of the interstate highways, but the first paving project completed under the 1956 Federal-Aid Highway Act was an eight-mile stretch of road west from Topeka, Interstate 70.

These highways make cross-country travel expedient. I-5 rides the West Coast from Mexico to Canada. The East Coast has I-95 from Miami to the Canadian border. I-10 runs from Los Angeles to Jacksonville, Fla. In the north, you'll find I-90, Seattle to Boston. Our own interstate, I-35, begins in Laredo, Texas, and ends at Duluth, Minn.

While interstates are not generally associated with beautiful scenery, there are many nice stretches. I-540, for example, between Fort Smith and Fayetteville, Arkansas, has pretty vistas. And I-70 west of Denver offers dramatic landscape (east of Denver, not so much).

As you are surely aware, one of the most gorgeous stretches of interstate highway is I-35 between Emporia and El Dorado, snaking travelers through the uncluttered beauty of the Flint Hills.

Next time you're zipping along on one of our country's fine interstate highways, give a nod to the one who helped to get the steamrollers rolling—the five-star general, the 34th president, the man from Kansas.

November 2005

SEED POTATOES

I found a thin white box at my dad's house. The box held sympathy cards that had been sent to our family 40 years ago when my grandfather died from a heart attack.

Most of the names signed were familiar to me. Cards came from Pawnee Rock residents, church members, my mother's family, from the superintendent of schools.

One card, sent by a fellow Mennonite, included a note on the back.

Rollie Schmidt wrote: "That was quite a shock for everyone to have Otis slip away so quickly. He gave us some seed potatoes once and we always appreciated that."

I love that last line.

In all likelihood, this transfer of seed potatoes was a casual event, but it apparently meant something to Rollie.

I was 6 years old when my grandfather died, so my memories are thin and wispy. But four decades later, I can still picture the weather-worn face of my grandfather; hear his clipped consonants and the sharp edges of that German accent.

Rollie's note refreshed my memories and it gave me access to a moment of Grandpa's life.

Most of the time, this is how we gather family history—in fragments.

We may stumble across a ledger, a postcard, a letter. Perhaps we learn something new from the writing on the back of a photograph. If I gathered together all the memories and the things I know about Grandpa, would I be able to fill a bushel basket?

Maybe.

Over time, if we're lucky, we hear and collect stories about our relatives. When I wrote to my brother about discovering these sympathy cards, Leon e-mailed a few of his own memories.

"Grandpa liked to sit on the porch swing and have Shep [the dog] lick his feet," Leon remembered. "He said it helped his arthritis."

"Grandpa's favorite music was 'Rock of Ages,' which he liked to play on the pump organ in the living room," Leon wrote.

Although I was young, I do have my own Grandpa memories.

I recall one summer night that I spent sleeping on my grandparents' fold-out couch. In the morning, when I raised my head over the arm of the couch I saw Grandpa a few feet away, eating breakfast in the dining room.

"Well, look who's awake," Grandpa said and he gave me his full attention.

During harvest, I climbed the red metal rungs of Grandpa's combine (I think I had help; it was a long way between rungs for a little girl). Together, he and I cut a couple of swaths of wheat.

Grandpa loved horses; he had once worked the fields with them. A set of shelves in the farmhouse displayed ceramic and plastic horses.

"You and I were throwing a beach ball around G&G's living room and I knocked over a ceramic horse and broke its leg," Leon wrote. "Grandma promised that Grandpa would be unhappy, and he was."

After Grandpa died, the farm felt lonely, but we grandkids stayed there more often to keep Grandma company.

Grandpa's brown field jacket still hung in its place on the dining room doorknob. And Grandma started wearing that coat in the winter when she walked to the mailbox, when she fed the chickens and gathered eggs. Years later, Grandma died. The farm was sold, the house torn down.

We can't know all the details about our ancestors and we don't need to know everything. But it's always fun to uncover new information—like Rollie's comment about the seed potatoes. Every detail helps to create a family history that we carry in our minds.

For most of us, all we have of our long-gone grandparents are fragments of their lives. Bits and pieces. Slivers.

But . . . maybe that's enough.

June 2003

DIGGING UP BONES

I never thought I'd be sucked in by genealogy. Then a few years ago, it hit me, "Hey what about all those dead people in my past?"

For others, this question may sound more like, "Who am I? Who are my people?"

My interest in family history waxes and wanes, but lately something had been picking at me. I couldn't remember the name of my grandfather's first wife. So on a recent trip back home to Barton County, in search of her gravestone, I wandered through the Mennonite cemetery.

I was about 30 when I learned this first wife had even existed. I stumbled across the information. Literally.

At my grandmother's burial in the church cemetery in 1990, I stepped back into a small stone dated 1919. The caption under the name "Lorena" read "wife of Otis Unruh." Now as far as I was concerned, we had, just moments before, put the wife of Otis Unruh into the ground.

The plot thickened.

It turned out that Grandpa's first wife, Lorena, died in childbirth. The infant also died. Grandpa then married Lorena's cousin, my grandmother, who naturally didn't want it remembered that she was Grandpa's second choice.

With this atom of information learned after my grandmother's death, I had a little more insight into who she was, her wounds and her perceptions. Now I better understood the family dynamics—and Grandma herself.

She enjoyed having her grandchildren spend time on the farm. She showed us how to reach under a hen for eggs and how to chase away the mean geese that she kept for whatever reason.

She played 10-point pitch with us until 3 a.m. We begged her to teach us how to say dirty words in German. And she did.

Most of the time it doesn't occur to me that ancestry affects me. I think that I am a shiny new person, made from scratch. But occasionally, phantom strands of family lure me into their nomad lives and suggest that my story begins long before I was born.

My dad had shown me photographs of our wide-eyed, somber ancestors. The men hid behind thick beards and the women wore enough fabric to drape a house. But the relatives didn't seem real until I investigated them on my own.

The journey of the Mennonites took them across the continents and centuries as they searched for a home, finally settling in Kansas. My grandmother's grandfather, Christian Schultz, traveled from Russia to America in 1874. Recently I came across a short personal history of him. In Russia, Christian was a blacksmith, wheelwright and a carriage maker.

This narrative by Galen Koehn mentioned my great-great-grandfather's seasickness on the ocean voyage and said that he cured his malady by eating rye bread. The article described his natural ability as a bonesetter and also gave Christian's story of his proposal to Helena:

"When he had made up his mind to ask her to be his bride, he started for the Rudiger home on foot. . . . When he entered the home he found his fair one sitting on the floor shelling beans."

Speaking in his native Low German, he asked, "Do you want me or not?" She replied, "I guess I will have to."

Suddenly, Christian became real for me. He had a story, a voice and a personality (such as it was).

While relatives on my dad's side are Germans from Russia, my maternal ancestors came from other countries. Like most people in the United States, I'm part-this and part-that. Ancestry can be a jumbled mess. Still, it is nice to know which jumbled mess I come from.

The religious, ethnic, and family histories give me an outline of who I am, but it's just an outline. I get to color in the rest.

October 2005

LEAVING HOME

It felt like the linoleum was being pulled out from under me.

I recently learned that a place which has kept me grounded, given me a lifelong sense of continuity, will soon be only a memory.

Home.

Six months ahead of their original plans, my dad and stepmom moved to Great Bend. They told me the house would be auctioned within a month.

The small, ranch-style residence in Pawnee Rock was a basement house when Mom and Dad carried Baby Cheryl home from the hospital in 1959. Dad finished the above-ground level about the time I started walking.

The house that Dad built kept our family warm and dry. Our home's wooden walls shielded us from January winds, saved us from falling out into the snow. When spring came, our first awareness of rain was often the tinny clinks heard on the metal roof vents.

One afternoon in 1974, as a covey of tornadoes swarmed around Pawnee Rock, the house provided an underground shelter for the family (excluding my brother, who was out with his camera).

I spent only one night alone at home. And that night, when I was 17, an October ice storm knocked out the power. Afraid of the creepy house noises, I stayed awake on the couch with the dog beside me, both of us getting colder as the damp night lingered.

Standing in the living room last week, I tried to absorb everything for the last time. I caught the sun's rays gleaming through the south picture window, and I listened for the clicking of the latch on the wooden screen door.

I smiled, thinking of our rat terrier, Patches. As winter sunbeams made their day trip across the floor, so did the dog, seeking a warm place to sleep.

Perhaps my favorite spot was a chair near the picture window. From there I could see a half-block to the east and know who was hanging out at the tennis court. Or I could look across the street to a wooded lot where I was certain I'd find Indian artifacts.

On this last visit, not wanting to forget a square foot of space, I snapped more than 300 photographs of the place.

I took pictures of the hiding places that Dad built into the kitchen table. When we pulled out the table's drawers, my brother and I discovered small cubbyholes. We kept our secret things there.

The snapshots will help me remember the striped linoleum on the basement floor and also the startling shade of purple that I painted my bedroom walls when I was in the seventh grade.

Photos showing holes in the ceiling tile in my brother's room will remind me of Leon's throwing-pencils-and-sticking-them-into-the-ceiling phase of his life.

On Leon's bedroom door are two darkened lines from Scotch tape. As a teenager, feeling a need to bring attention to the Fourth Amendment, Leon taped a copy of the Bill of Rights to his door, where it stayed for more than a decade.

And the crayon marks were cleaned off long ago, but one day when I was learning how to print, Leon walked through the hallway and said, "Uh-oh." On the bathroom door, "Cheryl" was written in green crayon. Mom said I burst into tears when the crime scene was discovered.

What the photos don't capture are the sounds: the grinding of the sump pump, the whoosh of flames as the gas furnace fired up, the loud click of the light switch in the hall.

And these pictures don't show the roasting of marshmallows over the kitchen stove, Scrabble games played on winter nights, the slammed doors, the silence, the teenage dramas. I don't really need photos; the memories are imprinted on my soul.

And, as for the house—well, it will never forget us either.

April 2009

THE SOUND OF (OLD) MUSIC

During Easter weekend, I caught some of *The Sound of Music* on television. But then the film got to the annoying part with its yodeling puppet show—and I was forced to turn away.

I've not watched the entire movie since I was young, but there are parts that I've always remembered: people running in the night, grassy mountainsides, wholesome children and a bright-eyed governess who seemingly had the ability to invent song lyrics without pause.

When the film was released in March 1965, I was 5, going on 6. One afternoon, my family of four squeezed into a car with a family of three and we traveled an hour from Pawnee Rock to Hutchinson to see the show.

As the littlest human being in the car, I didn't get my own seat but was passed from Mom's lap to Dad's. (This was back when children had free-range movement in vehicles, to which I say thank goodness that I never had to endure the trauma of being confined in a child-safety seat.)

The trip to see *The Sound of Music* was the first time I'd ever been inside a movie theatre. Children's films weren't marketed as they are now, and besides, our family was just not a movie-going family. (Note: my parents did take my brother and me to a second film, one year later, in 1966, *A Man for All Seasons,* but the only clear-cut memory I have from that show is the sound of the guillotine.)

So, in 1965, as a kindergartner, the theatre experience was new. For one thing, I hadn't expected the darkened room that you walked into off the street. In the dark I couldn't see the sloped aisle, but it tilted me forward. I felt as if I had suddenly grown the biggest, heaviest head on the planet. Walking downhill, top-heavy, I nearly fell into spontaneous somersaults.

We took our places; my dad lifted me up and sat me down. And the seat promptly folded me in half—knees in my face. Luckily, children are natural yogis, quite bendable. As a runt of a child, I was not heavy enough to counterbalance the spring-loaded seat; I'm guessing that Mom or Dad held the seat down for me during the entire show.

And I must have been wearing a dress, because I remember how the seat's bristle-like velvet felt on the back of my legs as I listened to "Raindrops on Roses" and "Sixteen, Going on Seventeen."

Now leap forward to 1995. I'm in the living room of my rented bungalow, walking past the TV set. On a news program there's a segment about the 30-year anniversary of *The Sound of Music*

Not only did I immediately recall the bristly folding seat, the sloped aisle and the Von Trapp family hiding in the night, but I had one of those moments that makes a person stop and freeze.

"Oh, man," I thought, "I can remember something from three decades ago."

So at 35, going on 36, I felt the first blush of aging, that moment of depressing realization that a large chunk of time was now behind me.

And even worse, during this recent Easter weekend, as *The Sound of Music* played on television, there sat on my desk an envelope from AARP, another reminder of the now larger chunk of time that I've accumulated. Yes, that cult of old people is stalking me. How did they find me? How did they know that I've lived for exactly five decades? Can they smell wrinkles? Or do they smell the fear?

Besides the intrusion, I was not exactly warmed by the detachment of this initial mailing a month before my 50th birthday. Rather than requesting one's membership and a $16 check, maybe AARP could, instead, just send a pleasant birthday card.

Something gentle and genial would be appreciated here!

And it wouldn't hurt, say, to include a complimentary note that acknowledges one's beauty or youthfulness or contributions to society.

Really, kindness is everything. Especially when you're 49, going on 50.

Childhood

April 2005

OH, BROTHER

"How old were you when you first used *idiom* without prompting?" my brother asked in an e-mail.

Leon's 8-year-old son, Sam, had used the word idiom while explaining something.

"Your children scare me," I replied. "They're smarter than I am."

"You're scared?" he wrote, "How do you think I feel, knowing that there are three smarter people living under my roof, and they're all younger than I am?"

That last sentence was a little unsettling. Leon was referring to family, his wife and two sons, but still, I felt the world crumble a bit—one of my lifelong beliefs was in jeopardy.

An unwavering fact in my life is that my big brother is the most intelligent person on the planet.

Leon is two years older than I am. When we were young, it was obvious that he knew everything. He could explain barometric pressure and the formation of clouds. He showed me how to cast a fishing line and how to do a lay-up on the basketball court.

My brother read constantly, not just *Mad* magazine, but also history and political science. He always knew that he would become a journalist.

Leon was in the fifth grade when he started his own weekly newspaper, the *Pawnee Rock Informer.* He first typed it with carbon paper, then used a gelatin hectograph, and finally acquired a mimeograph from a minister who had used it to print church bulletins. For more than three years, Leon reported city and school news in the *Informer* and delivered his newspaper to subscribers.

A good student, Leon represented Pawnee County one year

in the state spelling bee and he was a National Merit Finalist.

I idolized my brother. But we didn't always play well together. He often made me angry. Some days I hated him.

During childhood, we fought with words and sometimes fists. Brighter and stronger, Leon won every battle.

I don't know whether "ipit dipit" was his coined phrase or mine. When we were little kids, ipit dipit was the worst insult that we could fling without a scolding from Mom.

I still call him that occasionally, but now, of course, it's impossible to put any fury into those words.

My brother was everything I wanted to be. Because he was in 4-H, I couldn't wait to join the club. He played a coronet in band, so I took up the coronet as well.

Leon taught himself photography. At high school ballgames, he stood behind the basketball goal or at the 30-yard-line with the camera's viewfinder to his eye.

When my brother graduated, I took over his post on the football field sidelines and I leaned against the gymnasium wall, his heavy old Ricoh camera hanging around my neck.

He worked for *The Tiller and Toiler* newspaper in Larned. So did I. He went to the University of Kansas; I joined him a few years later.

About 10 years ago, before he had those sons who adore him, Leon enlarged a photograph showing the two of us as youngsters.

In the photo, my brother and I, at ages 5 and 3, are wearing Sunday clothes, standing in our front yard. Elm trees are leafed out and roses grow along the white picket fence. The sun shines on our hair.

Leon, a full head taller than me, rests his hand on my shoulder. My fingers reach up and grab that hand. His eyes and mouth are wide and happy and I am beaming at him as if he is a god.

When Leon gave me the photograph, he suggested that it captured the last time that anyone had looked up at him with such complete admiration.

His comment surprised me.

How could he have not seen that during my entire life I had admired him, emulated him, worshiped him every single step of the way?

What an ipit dipit!

August 2007

RIDING THE ROUTE

Out in the country, school buses are raising dust again. And they're cruising around town. One just drove past my house, carrying a thousand pounds worth of children.

It has been many years since I climbed aboard one of those yellow buses and walked through the canyon of green vinyl seats. Where I came from, only country kids rode the bus. I was a town kid but was lucky enough to ride because I had friends in high places—my dad was a bus driver.

For 18 years he drove bus No. 4 for the Pawnee Rock Schools. And at 4 years old, I was his youngest rider. On days Mom worked, my brother and I rode with Dad on his morning route. While my brother was in school, I tagged along with Dad all day, often riding in the afternoon as well.

Today, as the yellow buses lumber past my house, I'm pulled back to the 1960s, into that bus of yore, with its bench seats, the humps in the floor over the back wheels and the ratchet-like sounds of windows being raised.

On Dad's route, we crossed the Arkansas River and drove through the sand hills to stop at the Kasselman place. On the circle drive at the Mull family compound, I had to hold my nose because next to Glenn and Jeanine's house was their father's feedlot.

And somewhere south of town, we picked up the McGinnes kids—one of whom was Viola. I coveted Viola's multicolored sneakers. The cloth tops had a patchwork quilt design and were snazzier than my plain red Keds.

I learned the names of all the riders. Some were first-grade students, some high school seniors. At home, I studied their photos in the school yearbook.

These big kids probably thought of me as the little monkey

of a girl who tried out every seat in the bus, opened and shut windows and, more than likely, put paw prints and forehead prints on the glass.

Often I sat in the seat behind my dad to watch him drive, to see him extend the stop sign with his left hand and open the door with his right. A tilted mirror hung above the windshield and let him keep an eye on his passengers.

When a whoop or a holler came from the back of the bus, Dad's blue eyes shot up toward the mirror and the bus quieted without a word.

Over time, I came to know where each family lived, figured out which roads led to whose houses, and became familiar with the Etch A Sketch path of 90-degree turns that my dad made every day of the school year. Twice a day.

Perhaps those afternoon rides, listening to the chatter of junior high and high school students, made me feel a part of something bigger. As I watched these kids, I saw what I could become. And I wanted to be like the bright-eyed Jeanine Mull, whose brown hair fell across her face as easily as her smile.

You never know what will leave notches in a kid's mind. Maybe riding the bus helped me learn to love the grid of landscape, the furrowed fields, the soft hills on the Kansas plains.

We are merely an accumulation of our miles and of our days.

March 2003

ONE MAN'S TREASURES

Trying to reflect on something more uplifting than war, I've been thinking about my dad this week. Wednesday is his birthday.

He's one of those guys who collects anything rusted and worn out. Each time I visit, some of his old treasures wind up in my car.

My father operated a woodworking business for 46 years in downtown Pawnee Rock. On the walls in that shop, he displayed his various collections: numbered railroad nails, yardsticks, pop bottles, and barbed wire.

This woodworking shop was often my day-care center, dad my day-care provider. So, no, as a youngster, I did not spend my days in front of the television watching *Romper Room* and *Captain Kangaroo.* While he built cabinets and bookshelves, I swept sawdust from the concrete floor of his shop. And with his hand guiding mine, he taught me how to saw a board and hammer a nail.

On days when we hauled trash to the city dump, Dad and I kicked around in the dirt, looking for old bottles.

Occasionally we visited Chet Spreier's house at the edge of town. Now, Chet owned several lots of property filled with rusting farm machinery, tools, washboards and wire. I always thought of Chet as my dad's junk-collecting hero. They both had a ton of car tags.

In his woodworking shop, Dad displayed license plates on the high walls. Tags representing each of the 50 states hung in a colorful splash over a plate-glass window. Another wall showed a complete set of 1965, white-on-red license tags from every county in Kansas.

When Mrs. Latas, my sixth-grade teacher, demanded that we memorize the 105 Kansas counties and county seats, I had a head start, having studied Dad's alphabetical wall of metal, a periodic chart of sorts, from AL (Allen) County to WY (Wyandotte) County.

One time when I went home, Dad pointed to the endless array of car tags in his backyard and asked, "Need any old license plates?"

Well, *need* is not exactly the word that comes to mind.

My dad has always handed down bits and pieces of family items, but he became more eager to unload belongings after his near-fatal accident six years ago. As he crossed the street near his house, he was hit by a pickup, its driver blinded by the rising sun.

There was an ambulance, a helicopter, emergency surgery and a 12-day coma. My stepmother, Betty, who wouldn't settle for less than a complete recovery, pulled him back into the land of the living with prayer and fierce determination.

After a few months of convalescence, my dad, the father of all packrats, took a long look at what he had accumulated and realized that he had a second chance to thin out his collections.

So Dad's packrat offspring have been the beneficiaries.

My brother and I have each hauled to our respective homes several pieces of Grandma's furniture, leftover decorative metal from the fence that once surrounded Pawnee Rock State Park, lightning rods from Grandma's barn, a souvenir doorknob from Dad's shop.

I filled a glass cabinet with dried-up ballpoint pens from dried-up businesses in town, pocket knives from Farmer's Grain, Fuel & Livestock, coin banks from the long-gone Pawnee Rock State Bank.

This "junk" tells the story of my family, my hometown. To purge these gifts, to separate emotion from belongings, would feel like severing ties.

So, the packrat daughter keeps these things.

But what she values most is the time spent hanging out with her dad—learning how to hammer a nail and saw a board, and hunting for old bottles with him at the city dump.

August 2004

A WHIFF OF DILL

The moment that I stepped into Reeble's grocery store last week, I could smell it. Behind the tables of baked goods and near the onions and potatoes, 3-foot-high stalks of dill stood in a barrel.

I've heard that odors trigger memories so well because the olfactory cortex is next to the part of the brain that handles emotions and memories.

Upon inhaling the fragrance of fresh dill, I always become a time traveler, immediately flung decades into the past. I land abruptly at the door to the brooder house on my grandmother's farm. On tables in that otherwise empty brooder house, Grandma dried her homegrown dill.

During childhood summers in the 1960s, my cousins and brother and I made weeklong visits to our grandmother's farm northwest of Pawnee Rock. Summer days found us on some kind of adventure. One year, our attention was grounded in the clay pit. We scooped thick gray goop from between limestone layers in the gully that ran through the pasture. Our attempts to mold vases and bowls failed because the clay wouldn't hold together.

We helped out with the garden. And in the chicken house, Grandma let us reach under the hens to pull out the warm eggs.

In the afternoon, we walked a quarter-mile down the rutted driveway to see if the mailman had left letters or the weekly *Grit* newspaper.

We grandkids often climbed up the ladder that led to the barn's hayloft. When they were kids, my dad and my uncles played basketball on the barn's second floor. It didn't seem like an inviting court to us—especially with that hole in the floor near the free-throw line where the ladder came through from the ground level.

In the south end of the hayloft, we found a cat skeleton, which kind of spooked us. We wondered what could have killed it up there.

One year, when there weren't any cattle on the farm, the weeds in the corral were more than six feet high. Unlike most weeds, which are scratchy and harsh, these felt cool and soft.

We made tunnels through the corral, pressing down some of the weeds to make a cushioned floor and bending the tall stems over the tunnels to make a roof. I can still picture the blue sky showing through that green ceiling.

Fruit trees grew near the windmill behind the barn. Alongside Grandma, we climbed stepladders and stepstools in the draw, filling buckets with cherries and mulberries. Later, sitting at the kitchen table, our hands became wet and sticky as we pitted the cherries.

I think Grandma baked a pie every morning of her life. I often woke to the sound of her heels clomping in the kitchen. On the farm, my grandmother always wore a pair of scuffed black pumps. And she wore dresses that that she had sewn herself. This was her attire for corralling cattle, for weeding the garden and for baking pies.

Grandma sprinkled cinnamon and sugar on the pie dough scraps and baked them until they were delicate and golden brown. We treasured those treats more than the pies.

The cherry pie was eaten after a lunch of Grandma's fried chicken. "If it's not sweet enough," Grandma said about every single fruit pie she baked, "just lift up the top and add more sugar."

The time machine that transported me to the late 1960s and to my grandmother's farm was not high-tech—no lights or dials, no transport vessel. It was merely a bunch of dill, tied together, standing in a basket at Reeble's.

January 2009

KNOWING THE WORDS

The other day, a local radio station played a song that had been released in 1975—America's "Sister Golden Hair." I don't hear that tune very often but the melody brought the words right back to me, and I sang along in the car.

Music is a time machine. On the rare occasion that I hear a song by The Grass Roots, I feel like I'm 17 again. I rode to high school with a boy who played The Grass Roots' *Greatest Hits* on his 8-track player. Over and over.

Songs tuck themselves away into our subconscious minds. If "Sooner or Later" started playing right now, the lyrics would come from my mouth without even thinking about them.

Years and songs, well, they tend to pile up on us.

As I contemplated that piling up of music and time, my mind slipped back to an afternoon in the '60s in the basement of our home in Pawnee Rock. My 8-year-old fingers plinked the right-hand melody of "Beautiful Dreamer" on our old upright piano.

As I played the Stephen Foster song, Mom cut out a dress, her scissors grinding on the wooden table with each cut through the blue polyester fabric. Mom sang along with my erratic playing. She knew the words to "Beautiful Dreamer."

Our multipurpose room in the basement held the black-and-white television set, the piano, and Mom's sewing machine. This was not a cozy room; it had lime-green cinderblock walls and a sheet of linoleum covering the cement floor.

My parents had paid $10 for that piano, buying it used from the Pawnee Rock Christian Church. One afternoon I watched Dad lower the piano into our basement by tying a rope around it and around the tree just outside the back door. He eased it down the wooden stairway.

The piano wouldn't stay in tune, but I've never been able to hold a tune either. (Perhaps my vocal talents were led astray by that off-key instrument.) Some of the ivories were chipped or missing and the black paint had worn off the ends of the B-flat and F-sharp in the middle of the keyboard.

Nevertheless, I was delighted when the piano came into our basement and into our lives. I liked playing music, enjoyed turning notes into songs. I took piano lessons and was learning how to coordinate left and right hands. But after playing those lesson-book songs with their big black notes and child-aimed lyrics repeatedly, I longed for real music.

The songs in our hymnals had too many notes on each hand for me to play, but I found some easier songs. Mom had a music book with a hundred or so popular, but not necessarily current, American tunes.

My fingers found their awkward way through the melody line of "Battle Hymn of the Republic." Mom knew the words. I played "Oh! Susanna," "Onward Christian Soldiers" and "Greensleeves." Mom sang along.

When I played "Aura Lee," Mom told me that Elvis Presley had used that same tune for his song "Love Me Tender." So I played it again and she sang Elvis' lyrics.

"How can you know the words to every song?" I asked, marveling at my mother's obvious intelligence.

"Oh, you just hear the songs over and over and you learn the words," she explained.

Now sure, Mom was old (33!), but still, I couldn't imagine anyone having listened to hundreds of songs enough times to have memorized all the words to each of them.

The other day, as I sang along with the radio, old songs, new songs, one song after another, I thought about what Mom had said, and realized I had reached that place, the place where the words come easily.

Years and lyrics, they do pile up on you.

February 2003

SMALL TOWN, OLD FRIEND

Recently I ate lunch with a lifelong friend. I can't even guess how many childhood sentences began "Amy and I . . . ." We grew up in the same small Kansas town. We lived the same childhood.

Amy is a civil engineer in Kansas City and designs wastewater treatment plants. I'd like to think that her career inspiration came during our grade school days. Our town's sewage treatment plant sat at the smelly end of a quarter-mile road. We challenged ourselves to see how far we could walk toward it without gagging.

If you want to have fun in a small town, you have to make it yourself.

And we did.

Amy and I go way back, to the first image that I can retrieve. That memory, at age 2, is little more than a photograph in my head. However, most memories since then involve laughter or giggles (way too often during sermons).

Actually, our connection preceded our existence. Her ancestors and mine came from the same community in Russia. (Germans from Russia, long story.) Although we shared this background, our friendship developed by finding our own adventures. With only one fuzzy TV channel out of Wichita caught by an outside antenna (two channels if the weather gods were on our side), we spent little time on the couch.

Because we grew up during the 1960s and 1970s in a town of 400 residents, nearly all of our life experiences were shared ones. Together we trick-or-treated and Christmas-caroled and jumped off the roof of her chicken house (once).

During our lunch, Amy and I remembered those childhood

days, that in our town were both idyllic and insular. The rest of the world carried on without us. On the *NBC Nightly News*, Chet Huntley and David Brinkley announced the weekly body count from the Vietnam War. Men landed on the moon. We read about anti-war protests, the Kent State shootings, the kidnapping of Patty Hearst. The action happened a long way away (especially the moon landing). This isolation was exactly what made the town a quiet place where we happily wandered the streets, day or night.

As girls, our bikes stirred up dust on the streets of Pawnee Rock while we hunted for something to do. We tiptoed barefoot over sticker patches that encroached on sidewalks between our two homes. And on Sundays, the Saturday night broken beer bottles added more of a challenge to bare feet. Amy and I exchanged Nancy Drew books and would have given our middle names for a mystery to solve.

As adults, what impresses us in today's cautious world is that we had tremendous freedom—the run of the town by age 7 or 8. Even before we were teenagers, we walked to "the crick" or to the river, about a mile south of town. Our parents expected us to make wise decisions.

Except for a few incidents such as when our friend Sarah dropped a leg through the second floor of an abandoned building we shouldn't have been in, or when five of us 13-year-old girls were called over to the car of a stranger who thought it important to show us his private parts, our days were unmarred with danger.

Since we left town 25 years ago, buildings have been demolished and cottonwood and elm trees removed. When I visit, I'm always surprised that the town has changed and equally surprised that it hasn't.

The lunch with Amy ended after three hours and a gallon of iced tea. I'm thrilled that our friendship has grown up with us. Very few people lived those same years in Pawnee Rock, petted my dog Patches, and knew my parents when they were the same age that I am now.

Because Amy and I shared those thousands of small-town days, she understands parts of me that no one else ever will.

September 2008

DITCHED

When Rick Clawson, a former classmate from Pawnee Rock, contacted me recently, he and I discussed things we did for fun in our small town. As kids, we played hide-and-seek after dark, rode our bikes to the creek and explored the round barn.

Rick said in an e-mail, "I am never bored after growing up in Pawnee Rock. How could I be?"

I laughed when I read that, because it's true; living in a small town forces you to become resourceful. Other than Scouts and 4-H, there were no organized activities for kids in Pawnee Rock. We had no soccer, no softball, nothing.

But we small-town kids did have a couple things going for us. At birth we were each issued an imagination. And by age 5 or 6, most of us acquired a bicycle of some kind, likely a hand-me-down bike.

Equipped with those two things—an imagination and transportation—we had it all. We were inventive, we improvised, we entertained ourselves.

Then progress limited our assets. Sometime around 1970, city leaders shouted, "Out with the ditches! In with the gutters!"

I have no idea what spurred the upgrade; maybe the city mothers and fathers thought our dirt-street town lacked curb appeal. Perhaps there were drainage problems or the ditches were hatching too many mosquitoes, I just don't know. But they poured concrete curbs and gutters and one of our natural playgrounds was destroyed in the process.

We kids had made good use of those ditches. In wintertime, they filled with deep snow and we jumped in with both feet.

After a rain, my brother and I built dams in the ditch using mud, pebbles and twigs. My brother was the family's mud engineer and I'd float our bathtub boat in the brother-made lake.

Ditches made bike riding more fun. We'd ride bikes on the sidewalks and as we approached a street, it was fun to swerve and swoop into the ditch rather than stay on the sidewalk. When the curbs came in, out went our little bypasses.

My friend, Amy, and I had another use for the ditches. That was where we practiced "the Mannix roll."

As detective-wannabes, Amy and I were fond of that rugged private investigator on TV, Joe Mannix. Mr. Mannix found himself in dangerous situations every week. Thugs shot at him and chased him with their vehicles. Mannix was often seen bouncing off the hoods of cars or rolling out of the way a second before a vehicle's tires could smash him.

Between my house and Amy's, in front of Mrs. Carpenter's place, was a shallow ditch filled with a soft mat of crabgrass. We walked down the sidewalk nonchalantly, pretending things were normal, but when a Chevy or Ford approached on the street with a threatening evil-doer behind the wheel, Amy and I would shout "Hit the dirt!" then dive into the ditch, rolling in the grass. Sometimes Amy and I would crawl on our bellies in the ditch for the entire block, hiding from imaginary enemies.

By the third grade, we had outgrown *Dick and Jane* and Mrs. Dunavan handed out worn readers with frayed covers. These books offered stories of adventure.

We took those stories home in our minds. At Marilyn's house, my friends and I acted out the fictional stagecoach tales of Lightning Joe. He bravely transported folks westward, shielding them from attacks and trying to keep the coach from overturning when fording a stream.

So we girls acted out the stories, taking turns pulling each other in a red wagon along the sidewalk. "Yah! Yah!" Lightning Joe shouted as he snapped the whip. Then trouble came, as it always did, and the red wagon spilled its passengers into the ditch.

Into the lovely, grass-covered ditch.

July 2009

FIVE HUNDRED MILES

At summer camps across the state, children gather around campfires every evening. Slick with bug spray, sticky from melted marshmallows, those youngsters are singing songs like "This Little Light of Mine."

Kids, beware: Camp songs can ride your mind for the rest of your life. In 40 years, "Baby Bumble Bee" will still buzz in your brain like a man-eating mosquito.

Once learned, you will never forget "Great Green Globs of Greasy Grimy Gopher Guts" because not only is it a favored gross-out song, but that lovely literary tool of alliteration also makes lyrics way too easy to remember.

But the tune that always takes me back to the banks of the Ninnescah River is the melancholy "Five Hundred Miles." Standing at the campfire's edge under a midnight-blue sky, a counselor strummed his guitar and put just the right amount of longing into being 500 miles from home.

Some camps are held indoors, such as basketball, cheerleading, computer and music camps. But many are set in the wilderness, where kids meet spiders and snakes—sometimes in the bathhouse, much to one's surprise in the middle of the night.

I think I was 10 years old the first year I went away to camp. My friend, Amy, and I had saved our allowances for church camp and our parents paid the rest. Then they hauled us a hundred miles to Camp Mennoscah near Murdock in Kingman County (Mennonites + Ninnescah River = Camp Mennoscah).

It's easy to romance the concept of summer camp, but honestly, I don't know why I ever thought it would be a good idea. Back then I was incredibly shy. And if I had known that Amy would not be with me 24/7 (she was assigned to Moonbeam cabin; I was in Starlight), I might not have been so eager to sign up.

Shyness was a curse. Starting a conversation with a stranger was nearly impossible. And I also blushed easily, which brought negative attention. Because my face was often crimson, I became grateful for sunburns, which provided camouflage.

Luckily, the seven or eight other girls in my cabin were friendly. As we chose our bunks, Sheila broke the ice by demonstrating her ability to recite the alphabet while belching. She gave lessons. And Jean from Moundridge became a friend and later a pen pal, one I would write to for the next five or six years.

Those seven days held moments of anxiety, but there were also times when I felt at home. And then there was the pool incident.

I took to camp a never-worn, two-piece swimsuit. This was back in the 1960s, so think double-knit, thick polyester. When I jumped into the small pool, I discovered that the swimsuit took on water like a towel.

Apparently I didn't yet have a grasp of physics because I climbed out of the pool to make my first dive. I ran down the gritty board, took a little bounce and dove off the end; my body sliced cleanly through the water. The force of entering the pool pulled the water-heavy swimsuit bottoms right off my hips—a moment of pre-teen horror if ever there was one.

Thankfully, the swimsuit tangled at my ankles instead of floating to the surface. As I frantically pulled up the bottoms, I felt heat rush to my face; I blushed underwater. When I surfaced, no one was pointing or laughing, so apparently the secret was mine. But that traitorous swimsuit could have been the end of me. Thereafter, I wore a T-shirt over the suit and gave up diving.

I returned to Camp Mennoscah the following year and later attended a Girl Scout camp as well as Rocky Mountain Mennonite Camp. I worked at making friends—and bought a trustworthy swimsuit.

Camp presented challenges for a shy kid, but the painful and embarrassing moments were balanced out by the good times, especially the campfires and singing together under the stars. As the glow of the fire landed upon our faces, we felt unified and connected—because all of us were, in one way or another, five hundred miles away from home.

January 2009

COOKING FOR BOYS AND GIRLS

While doing some Christmas shopping in Town Crier Bookstore, I stumbled upon *Betty Crocker's Cook Book for Boys and Girls*. This book is a reproduction of the 1957 cookbook that my brother, Leon, and I had when we were growing up.

Now I don't know if Leon used the cookbook much, but I tried some of the recipes when I was a batter-licking little girl. I made Black Cat Cookies, Good Kid Cookies and Raggedy Ann Salad.

With illustrations on every page and many color photographs, the cookbook was and is a great way to teach children about food preparation. It shows how to set a table, explains how to measure flour and vanilla, and defines terms such as mince, dice, and toss.

It was fun to look at the cookbook again and see how things were back in the 1950s. Illustrations show girls wearing dresses and aprons while baking. In the book, a boy says that he made a cake for his father and "Dad said it was keen."

The cookbook is loaded with pictures of faces. Cookies have faces, cupcakes have faces. Raisin eyes and mouths are placed on pears and peaches.

And Betty Crocker even suggests placing a prune in a bowl of Wheaties and using apple bits to create facial features on the prune. When you're a kid, it really is all about playing with your food.

Maybe the book was published before the widespread use of blenders, or perhaps Betty Crocker didn't want kids using power tools, because when a drink recipe called for crushed ice, the book said to put ice cubes in a plastic bag, wrap the bag in a newspaper and pound it with a rolling pin or a hammer.

Yes, boys and girls of today, that's the way we used to cook—with a hammer.

My mother worked outside the home, but she taught my brother and me to be self-reliant. Therefore, we were perfectly capable of feeding ourselves when she was gone or busy. One snack I relied on was ketchup sandwiches. (Take one slice of white bread, pour on ketchup, fold and eat.) That recipe wasn't in the cookbook.

Pop Tarts were invented in 1963, during my childhood, but were not a regularly available item at our house. We ate cereal for breakfast: Cap'n Crunch was a favorite, and I liked Sugar Smacks and Alpha-Bits. (Spelling for breakfast, a brilliant idea.)

Mom often boiled eggs for us and left them in the refrigerator. My brother and I took those hard-boiled eggs to new heights. We climbed onto the kitchen chairs and dropped the eggs to the floor, where they landed on their paper towel targets. It worked. The shells cracked. I wasn't fond of actually eating the eggs, but cracking the shells sure was fun.

When we were old enough to be trusted with fire, Leon and I cooked hot dogs before going to school. In order to cook on our gas stove, we'd take a kitchen match, set it ablaze by sticking it into the pilot light, an open flame in the center of the stove top. Then we turned on the gas and lit the burner with the match.

We fried hot dogs in a skillet, and even now I prefer my mine with a little crusty blackness on them rather than eating blandly boiled wieners.

In the mid-1970s, Mom purchased a microwave oven; we may have been the first family on our block to have one. During a junior high slumber party, part of the entertainment was watching frozen burritos cook in the new microwave.

Meal preparation has changed quite a bit in the past 50 years. Nowadays, I doubt that any kid eats prunes on his Wheaties. I can't imagine that many girls wear dresses while baking cupcakes. And many refrigerators now dispense crushed ice, eliminating the need for hammers in the kitchen.

Hard-boiled eggs, however, still should be dropped from a height of approximately five feet in order to properly crack their shells.

November 2008

DIALING THE PAST

There's a brand new cell phone tucked into my jeans pocket.

It's about the size and shape of a deck of cards—half the bulk of my previous phone. It flips open, it flips shut. I can use it to take photographs and send text messages. It has a calculator, a calendar, an alarm clock.

Even though I generally avoid phones, I'm pretty excited about this new toy. And as I observe kids walking down the sidewalks, their thumbs jumping around on the keypads of their phones, I feel a bit wistful for the past, because a cell phone would have been a life-changing thing for me as a kid.

If my best friend, Amy, and I had had cell phones when we were youngsters, we could've relayed messages to each other while pretending to be detectives like Nancy Drew.

It's easy to imagine myself as a girl, at bedtime, sending a text message to Amy, who lived two blocks away. And I can picture the two of us, sitting side-by-side in a pew, punching out messages to each other during sermons. I can also visualize those phones being confiscated by our mothers.

But, of course, in the 1970s, cell phones were not around. Heck, back then in my hometown of Pawnee Rock, the operator had to connect long distance calls for us. We didn't have push button phones, or answering machines, or cordless phones or caller ID.

Back in those ancient days, Amy and I did the best we could. We constructed a tin-can telephone: two empty cans with a string pulled tight between them.

Yeah, that didn't work.

So Amy and I sometimes left secret messages on paper in

designated spots. I remember finding one mysterious note cleverly signed, "Amynonymous."

Phones are simply tools of communication, a way to connect, and connection is what I desired so strongly back then.

Most of my good friends had a sister, so they had a constant companion, someone to play Monopoly with, or bake cookies with, someone to fix their hair. And I often felt left out. Me, well, I had a brother, and we played soccer, football and basketball in the yard. Leon taught me how to cast a fishing line and repair bike tires, and after school we sat in our basement eating Fudgsicles while watching *Major Astro* on TV.

Those were good times with Leon, but it just wasn't the same as having a sister.

So I spent a lot of time alone. I filled that time by reading books and newspapers. I rode my bike around town, went to the Post Office to check for mail, and stopped in at the grocery store for Jolly Ranchers—because it was my job to keep the dentist in business.

As a kid you do what you can to entertain yourself—I memorized the lyrics of every Jackson 5 song, practiced basketball lay-ups, measured out 50 yards so I could dash in the street. I wrote ghastly poetry.

And most days, I would've given anything to have had that connection to friends that a pocket phone would've offered. Back in those days before cell phones, before the Internet, we had to entertain and amuse ourselves. And, actually, those were pretty good skills to develop.

Still . . . my gosh, it would've been so absolutely cool to send secret messages to Amy, punching letters into my phone, in the dark, from beneath the covers.

May 2005

WHAT MOTHERS DO

Chances are I've never met your mother.

It's a big world, after all, and I'm just a quiet and somewhat introverted person. Nevertheless, I'll bet that I can name a few things your mother did for you while you were growing up. In fact, I've made a list.

Yeah, well, OK, this is a list of things that *my* mother did for *me*. But, maybe your mom did similar things.

A mother hauls you and your friends eight miles to Larned to the nearest swimming pool. After she runs her errands, she waits in a hot car under the shade of an elm tree to let you swim for "just five more minutes, please."

Then, on the way home, she stops at the Dairy Queen and buys treats for you and your shivering friends.

A mother shows you that in order to detangle your hair, you comb gently from the ends and work in toward the knot.

A mother lets you pout when you are 11. And 12, and 25, and 42.

She doesn't scold you for picking every single grape hyacinth in the front yard.

A mother teaches you countless things: how to play tennis, how far apart to plant lettuce seeds, and how to pull ticks off of the dog.

When your cat gets its head stuck in a mayonnaise jar, a mother manages to break the jar without injuring the frightened kitty.

She buys a piano. And is brave enough to be in the house while you learn to play. And actually says she enjoys listening.

When you're in the eighth grade, a mother rushes to the hospital after she learns that you've been taken there with a broken arm.

When you enroll in Spanish class, she tells you that she, too, took Spanish in high school. She remembers the first line from her textbook: "¿Qué es el burro?" And now you will never forget that particular line either. It will come up in future conversations.

A mother introduces you to Mexican food, and searching for the best Mexican restaurants becomes a lifelong habit.

A mother rushes to the hospital again (this time on her birthday) when she gets the call that your face has accidentally been doused with watered-down hydrochloric acid during high school chemistry class.

She teaches you how to sew a dart, how to match plaids, how to put a zipper in a garment. And she shows you how to rip out seams when you sew them incorrectly.

She puts vitamin tablets at your place at the table.

A mother peels oranges for you for breakfast because you won't get around to eating them if you have to peel them yourself. (She doesn't call you lazy, although that term would certainly apply.)

When you get your wisdom teeth removed, she purees Spanish rice in the blender for you.

She lets you experiment with food coloring, even if the cake frosting turns out purplish-gray (repeatedly.)

She insists that you fasten your seatbelt.

A mother is the one you *don't* call because you know she'll detect that "something's wrong" from the sound of your voice.

A mother is the one you *do* call because you know she'll detect that "something's wrong" from the sound of your voice.

And, if your mother was anything like my mom, she loved you, unconditionally, even when you begged for "five more minutes," even when you picked every grape hyacinth, even when you pouted.

May 2008

HIGHWAY 71

The few times I've driven on U.S. Highway 71, I've felt a little guilty. The creation of the 71-bypass around Fayetteville, Arkansas, in the 1960s brought grief to my maternal grandparents.

I was just a small girl, but I knew that the highway (well, the government) was taking their land and that they were going to have to leave their farm.

When Grandma mentioned a difficulty they were facing because of the proposed road, she'd add, "That darned Highway 71," in a voice that sounded sometimes angry, sometimes defeated. Their house wouldn't be paved over, but the road was to cut through their property and they weren't willing to live that close to the highway.

Recently, on a return trip from Hot Springs, Ark., instead of driving the usual route through Oklahoma, I took I-540 north toward Missouri. In Fayetteville, I-540 follows the same route as Grandma's nemesis, Highway 71. At the south edge of Fayetteville, I exited the interstate and immediately came upon what I was looking for: Dowell Memorial Cemetery.

When I was a youngster, Dowell Cemetery seemed like a forgotten graveyard, lost in the middle of deep, dark woods. The cemetery was a short trek down the dusty road from my grandparents' small farm, which they owned during the 1950s and 1960s.

Much has changed in the 40 years since I was a regular visitor to this area. Dowell Cemetery is probably the only surviving landmark. And I'll bet it remains only because cemeteries are so dad-gummed difficult to move.

When I pulled off the interstate the other day, I drove beyond the cemetery on the road that once led to my grandparents' home.

It was now paved, and I drove only a few hundred yards before I overlooked the four-lane highway: 71.

Grandpa had built their house himself in 1953. It was a low-level, low-budget home several miles southwest of Fayetteville, near the Boston Mountains.

That little home in the country was a sweet place. Huge shrubs along the road hid their house from view. Out in back was Grandma's wildflower garden. And under the shade of hickory trees, Grandpa kept rows of rabbit hutches.

It was a place where good memories formed. In the evenings we sat in the backyard, talking over the sounds of insects and frogs.

I was tucked in for the night in the front bedroom under a pink and lavender-striped bedspread, and owls hooted me to sleep. In the mornings, Grandma made pancakes and sausage and served sliced peaches in tiny, colorful bowls.

But in these intervening 40 years, trees had been cut, mountains moved, concrete poured. Nothing looked the same. The woods had been turned into a four-lane highway. It's as if Grandma and Grandpa's place had never existed.

My grandparents relocated to Siloam Springs. As far as I know, they didn't hold a grudge. Still, I knew it had been a difficult event for them and so, as an adult, I felt a stab each time I had the occasion to drive on U.S. 71.

Grandma and Grandpa died in the 1970s and they were buried right here in Dowell Cemetery, just down the road from their old farm. The cemetery, once out in the boonies, was now adjacent to a huge highway interchange.

This was the first time I had visited my grandparents' graves, and I had a short, one-sided conversation with them. I sat on the ground in front of their headstone, used a twig to dig out some dirt stuck in the carved letters of their names. I admired the tiny wildflowers growing near the headstone. Grandma would've been pleased about the flowers.

The gulf of years had changed many things: the land had been rewritten, my grandparents were dead, I was getting older.

Back in the car, I suddenly felt proud to drive on that darned U.S. Highway 71. My grandparents had made their contribution; a piece of that highway belongs to me.

October 2007

GRANDMA'S QUILT

I had my head in the closet, swapping short sleeves for long ones, when I noticed the quilt.

"Ah, Grandma," I said to myself and smiled.

My grandmother didn't make the quilt specifically for me, but I somehow ended up with it—one of the few things I have that belonged to her. I've never even used this quilt. I've kept it hidden away so that it doesn't get dirty or stained or torn.

It was made by my Arkansas grandma, my mom's mom, whom my family visited once or twice a year when I was a kid. Even though her home was eight hours away, she was the grandparent I felt closest to.

I wish she had lived into my adult years; she died in her sleep when I was 18. But, in her last year of life, widowed, she moved from Arkansas back to her childhood hometown, Kinsley.

I spent the night with her in Kinsley on her June birthday in 1977 and it was just Grandma and me. Because I had only seen her during family visits, this was one of the few one-on-one times we ever had together. In her apartment, she and I sat at her small dining table and talked—about my summer job at the Larned newspaper, about my getting ready to start college in the fall, about my future.

"Whatever you do, Cheryl," Grandma told me, "keep writing."

If she only knew what those words have meant to me over the years.

We finished our meal and Grandma cut a pumpkin pie she had baked. As she transferred a slice from the pan to a dessert plate, the piece splashed into her glass of iced tea.

She laughed. We both did.

The other day when I pulled her quilt from the closet, all the Grandma memories came with it.

It's a crazy quilt, made with fabric remnants, odd-shaped blocks, fitted together like a puzzle. Each block is outlined with Grandma's needlework, a feather stitch of thick black thread.

Many of these scraps are familiar; the pieces were leftover material from some of grandma's dresses. She wore mostly muted colors. I remember the dress that was dollar-bill green, and the brown paisley one; swatches of both are sewn into the quilt.

And one piece of fabric that is scattered throughout the quilt is material from a dress she made for me. I called it my circus dress—because it had line drawings of animals and circus performers on the red and tan striped fabric. I wore that dress for my kindergarten picture.

Running my hand over this quilt reminds me of the times spent with my mom and my grandma in the fabric stores. Grandma couldn't pass up a dry goods store, which was fine, because my mom sewed a lot, too, and Mom was teaching me how to sew.

In these stores, I learned from watching Mom and Grandma that you can't walk past a bolt of cloth without reaching a hand out to feel the material.

They taught me about weight and texture and the wrinkle factor. They explained that lightweight cotton would work best for the gathering required on a peasant blouse, and that slick fabrics could sometimes be difficult to run through a sewing machine.

When I look at Grandma's quilt today, I see things that no one else can see. I see the fabric stores, Grandma's dresses and all the clothes that she made for me. I recall some of our conversations and the time that an errant piece of pumpkin pie made us laugh.

Intended or not, that crazy quilt comes with a personal history sewn right into it.

It's not going back into the closet. This winter, I'll throw it across my lap when I sit in the recliner to read. And now, with Grandma's quilt draped over the back of my chair; it feels as if she's dropped by for a visit.

Small Towns

January 2007

A TOWN BY ANY OTHER NAME

"Flush?" I asked. "What kind of name is that for a town?"

Dave and I saw the highway sign a few miles east of Manhattan while driving to a holiday dinner. Because we had already dawdled along the way, we skipped the seven-mile drive to Flush.

My sister-in-law, Nancy, is a native of Pottawatomie County, and I asked her about Flush when we arrived for dinner.

"Yeah, that's the name of the place," she said, adding that the founder was named Floersch. The Post Office Department apparently had trouble with the spelling, so they called it Flush. There's not much left there, Nancy said, besides a Catholic church, its rectory and cemetery.

When I returned home, I looked up Flush in the book *Kansas Post Offices* by Robert Baughman. Flush maintained a post office from 1899 to 1927. Its first appointee was Henry J. Floersch.

This past week I've spent a little time with that post office book. It lists over 4,000 names for post offices that were established between 1828 and 1961. That doesn't mean there were 4,000 communities; many towns had more than one name in their histories.

Fifty-two post offices existed in Lyon County during those years, but those 52 included name changes; there were only 46 towns.

Statewide, Olpe would surely win the identity-crisis prize. The community began as Bitlertown on Jan. 20, 1880. Then it became Olpe. There must have been a tug-of- war over names because it flip-flopped between Bitlertown and Olpe five times between 1880 and 1887.

Towns in the 1800s didn't have much of a shelf life. People

were transient, and many towns lasted only a few years. Communities often dissolved if the railroad bypassed them.

Among those post offices of days gone by was Cairo in Pratt County. Douglas County had Calcutta. For five years, Jerusalem was a post office in Johnson County, closing in 1900.

You could visit Chicago in Sheridan County. Sedgwick County once had El Paso (now Derby) and Waco (previously called Cowskin). And who knew that Valley Forge was in Smith County?

Bagdad and Key West were Coffey County towns. You'll still find Peru in Chautauqua County and Havana in Montgomery County. Coffey County was also home to Eclipse and Hardpan. Kingman County had a Butterfly and there was a Stranger in Leavenworth County.

In the past few years, Dave and I have visited several shadowy towns. While driving around them, we've joked about the movie *Deliverance.* Some places just feel like trouble—you sense that there's probably a methamphetamine lab in an abandoned house and a gun pointed at you through a broken window.

So I smiled when I learned that there once was a town called Deliverance. The word *deliverance* usually has positive connotations, and this long-gone Osborne County town had previously been called Pleasant Plain.

Dickinson County had Haphazard, the community of Example was set in Haskell County, and, in 1900, if you were looking for Success, Russell County would've been the place to go.

At one time, Decatur County had a Saint John—but its name was changed to Hooker.

Kansas has had towns called Sun (now Sun City), Sunbeam and Sunday. There were a couple of Sunsets, one Sunshine and two short-lived Sunflowers. The state had a Windhorst and a Zephyr.

Kansas Post Offices is simply a book of lists: names, dates and locations. But those lists took my mind down dusty trails and let it wander through some of those ghost towns with the colorful names.

September 2009

SMALL-TOWN EXPLORATION

While traveling around the Sunflower State, you pass through a lot of small towns. You can't avoid them, actually; like stars in the sky, they're everywhere. More than 500 of the 627 incorporated Kansas towns have fewer than 2,000 residents.

As you, my dear readers, surely know by now, I'm quite fond of small towns because I was raised in one, and, well, you just can't take the dirt-street-town out of the girl. But even people who did not grow up in a stoplight-free town can find these communities fascinating.

If you're not already sold on the idea of investigating them, let me help, let me be your guide to small-town exploration. I'll be glad to share with you what I look for when I pull into a Kansas town.

There's a lot you can discover about a place in as little as 20–30 minutes. That's right—you can play detective, gather facts and evidence, and make accurate (or maybe faulty) deductions. Even if you don't speak with any residents or tour the town's historical museum, you can get a feel for the community's personality and its history, just by observation, just by paying attention.

OK, here we go. To start, I look for a welcome sign. An attractive sign shows that residents care enough about their place to make a good first impression.

Slogans on those signs give a clue as to what the town is or wants to be. Florence proclaims that it is "Nestled in a valley of opportunity." And Lehigh: "Small, but it's home."

What is the town's overall appearance? Are the lawns well kept and junk free? Is the downtown tidy? If so, the residents probably have pride in their community and work together well.

Take a look downtown. Main Street might be three blocks long, full of stores—or maybe there are only two active businesses in town (and if so, I'm betting that one of them is a tavern).

Many business districts have the traditional two-story structures. These buildings may boast dates that go back to the early 1900s, maybe the late 1800s. While these may not have been the first structures in town, they give you a setting for the town's early days.

Study the town's architecture as a whole. Do a number of buildings appear to have been constructed during a particular decade? If so, that may indicate a boom time for the town.

Of course, this boom time concept works better with larger communities, but if a town has a surprising number of 1960s buildings, it might be reasonable to consider that a new industry came to town during that decade. Look around to see if you can support that theory with evidence.

Is the depot still in place? Does it appear that railroading was a major part of the town's history?

Some towns have murals with vignettes that recognize railroads, agriculture or other significant pieces of the town's history, and you can glean information that way.

Is there a pattern to the naming of streets? Some street names indicate the town's initial focus or even the background of its first residents. The German-settled community of Ellinwood, for example, has streets named Goethe, Wilhelm and Fritz.

To learn more about a town's heritage, visit the cemetery. Check the dates on the oldest headstones to determine when the town was established. If you see names that are, say, Czech, Swedish or German, you'll get an idea of the cultural background of the early residents.

What does the community recognize and remember? Towns often preserve pieces of history in a park or on public grounds. Many towns have saved an old school bell or the cornerstone of a church.

Did the town raise a famous resident? A roadside park in Burdett pays tribute to Clyde Tombaugh, discoverer of Pluto. Did something important happen in town? Dexter has Helium Memorial Park. Natural gas found underground there in 1903 was later determined to be helium.

A few minutes of thoughtful observation can give you a sense of the place and a hint of its history.

So there you go. That's some of what I look for in a small Kansas town. Your turn.

November 2004

THE OUTHOUSE TOUR

Kansans are resourceful. Use what you have—that's the Kansas way. Some people weave wheat into decorative windmills. A business in western Kansas sells tumbleweeds over the Internet.

If you have lemons, you make lemonade. If you have outhouses, well, um . . .

Down in Elk County, each year on the Friday and Saturday before Thanksgiving, the community of Elk Falls (pop. 110) invites the world to take a look inside their not-so-Porta-Potties.

It's a bargain and an adventure. For $1, you get a map and a voting ballot. A self-guided tour takes you around the heart of the town, peeking into other people's privies, about a dozen outhouses altogether.

"We'll have about 600 votes by the end of the day," Dorothy Tiffany said on the second afternoon of the two-day event. Tiffany was taking the dollars and handing out "Tour de John" buttons. She's been a volunteer at the outhouse tour since the event began nine years ago.

"Attendance was low yesterday because of the rain," Tiffany said. "Today we've had Red Hat ladies from Wichita and the Harper-Anthony area."

"This is the other serious thing we do," she said to an outhouse tourist as she held up a quart-size jar of small rocks. "This is guaranteed antique gray gravel and for 50 cents, you can put it into the pothole of your choice."

Behind the town's post office is Priority Privy. A ZIP Code directory is the reading material. Posted on the door: "Through rain and hail and sleet and snow, sometimes the postmaster has to go."

One outhouse pays tribute to a former resident, actor Barry McGuire (who played in the 1977 movie *Mary White*). Another had a deer-hunting theme with oak leaves for toilet paper. Next to the Quilts and More store, an outhouse was named The Quiltreen.

An outhouse at the Keefe homestead is called The Eleanor.

During the 1930s, in addition to other construction, the Works Progress Administration built outhouses. A flier available in the Keefe outhouse read, "In Republican areas such as Elk County, not everyone approved of such government assistance from Washington, although it gave employment to families who otherwise would have been on welfare. The critics called the WPA houses 'Eleanors' in honor of the First Lady."

My favorite outhouse was the Prayer Closet behind the Calvary Chapel. A tiny stained-glass window was built into the door. Inside, a jug of water was secured above a ceramic sink and painted on the sink were these words, "Create in me a clean heart, O God. Psalm 51:10."

After touring the town on foot, Dave and I settled in for lunch at the Village Café, a tiny restaurant in a converted house.

"This is like the Sistine Chapel," Dave said when we walked in the door.

"How so?" I asked, glancing around at the picnic tables and the wooden shingles on the interior wall.

"Up there," he said.

With rafters supporting the picture frame, parallel to the floor was a sofa-size reproduction of the arms-reaching-out section of Michelangelo's "The Creation of Adam."

We stopped at a quilt show in the Calvary Church and an arts and crafts show in the old gymnasium (built by the WPA). In the gym, I met an engaging young woman, Marie Greene, a soap-maker with Elk Falls Soap Co. I bought a bar of pearberry soap and commented on its wonderful fragrance.

"You should smell my house when the soap is curing," she said

Before leaving town, Dave and I visited the 1893 iron bridge that crosses the Elk River and overlooks the falls for which Elk Falls is named.

Elk Falls is proud of what it is—a tiny town with a sense of humor—and more than its share of outdoor plumbing.

May 2007

NO PLACE LIKE HOME

You know, I wish it had been someone other than Dorothy who etched this line into our consciousness, but . . . "There's no place like home."

Home has been on my mind as I think about the folks from Greensburg who have lost neighbors and friends, their houses and belongings and, well, their entire town, all in one frightening evening.

On May 4, one of the biggest tornadoes this country has seen in eight years nailed Greensburg, a town of about 1,400 people. When the storm pulverized the town, it was not selective; it took everything. Nearly every single building was blown to bits.

As the tornado stole the town from over their heads, residents fought for their lives in the hail-pounding, rain-soaked winds of death. Eleven lives were taken by the tornado.

From here on out, May 4 on the calendar will be like those white crosses placed in a highway ditch, the crosses that silently state: Lives were lost here.

About the only thing residents were left with is uncertainty. Should they rebuild? Will others return? Can this ever feel like home again?

Familiar surroundings are gone—the dresser covered with pennies, the open window over the kitchen sink, the chair the cat slept on.

When they least expect it, something will trigger an odd memory and they'll remember that groaning electric clock that never quite kept time, the old-wood smell of the antique bookcase and the way morning light landed on the dining room table.

The elm trees and backyard fences are gone. Porch swings, bicycles and flower gardens. The post office mailboxes, a candy rack at the drug store. Even stop signs are gone.

Temporarily, anyway, "home" is missing.

The word *home* is bigger than a house. Home is a well-worn neighborhood.

It's the school and the team mascot, churches, the tables where friends gather for coffee. It's the guy down the street who stops to visit as he walks his dog in the evenings.

Home is the route through town that you take every single day. It's that low spot between the trees, where you turn your eyes each morning to catch the pink sunrise.

Greensburg has lost much of its tangible history—the buildings that housed a succession of businesses, homes that had passed through generations of residents. Those old buildings stored psychic memories—the lingering presence of people who once lived and worked there. And no amount of rebuilding can bring that Greensburg back.

Residents will grieve many losses—the loss of life, of familiarity, the loss of continuity.

There are times in life when your world changes, not by choice, but by chance. And it's a chance we all take, living here in tornado alley. We think of Greensburg, Hoisington, Haysville, Andover, Hesston—and we know that next time, it could be us.

Greensburg residents will rebuild because Greensburg is home. They will replace street signs, plant trees, rebuild the school. And they will do this with help from the rest of us.

The boundaries of Greensburg now extend beyond the city limits, beyond Kiowa County. Kansas is one community. And here, we take care of our own.

June 2007

NOTES FROM THE WEST

One of the best things about a trip to Colorado is the drive through western Kansas.

I'm serious.

Western Kansas gets a bum rap, but the land is long and lean and its small towns are welcoming islands that rise from an ocean of wheat.

In May, Dave and I traveled to Colorado on U.S. 50 and returned home on U.S. 54. There was not a moment to rest my eyes, because there was so much to see.

In Abbyville, west of Hutchinson, residents were preparing for a rodeo. A sign announced that Friday was "tough enough to wear pink night."

Tornado damage from the May 4 and 5 storms could be seen along U.S. 50 in Stafford County. Shredded trees and belly-up irrigation systems showed the path of the storm.

One might assume that the Edwards County Courthouse would be in Kinsley's downtown business district. But no, the courthouse is north of U.S. 56 in a residential neighborhood.

While standing on the brick Main Street of Spearville, if you look to the north, you'll see white wind turbines. A wind farm quietly churns the air just outside of town.

The dome on the 1907 Carnegie Library (now Art Center) in Dodge City looks a lot like the dome on Emporia's Anderson Library. I later confirmed that the buildings had the same architect. Not surprisingly, there's a Gunsmoke Street in Dodge City. Dodge also has these businesses: Trails West True Value, Wild West Car Wash and Wyatt Earp Liquor.

In Cimarron, teenagers hang out at a classic soda fountain in Clark's Drug Store.

There are hills in western Kansas. Ingalls, in Gray County, is not a flat town.

From Garden City, we took a brief diversion to the north. Finney and Scott counties have enormous feedlots, but there are also some large dairy farms.

Wheat is planted to the edge of the sandy roads here. Jackrabbits pause in pastures. Your eyes take flight as a ring-necked pheasant flies from a ditch.

An unincorporated community in Scott County is called Shallow Water. The school is closed but the elevator is still in business.

Monument Rocks in Gove County has towers of beautiful chalk formations. There's no hoopla, no tour guide, no commercialization of nature's work. It's a quiet and surreal Kansas landmark rising from the range, making one ask, "How did this get here?"

Returning from Colorado, we passed through Johnson City, where a bank's marquee scrolls the closing grain prices.

In Haskell County, we came across land without ripples or hills. Here, with certainty, we could proclaim that we'd finally found flat land in Kansas.

The town of Satanta, named after the Indian chief, has streets named for tribes: Seminole, Ponca, Kaw, Wichita, Mohawk, Cheyenne, Sioux.

In Meade, numerous signs promoted the hideout of the Dalton Gang. "With all the arrows pointing toward it, it sure makes for a lousy hideout," Dave said.

A meadowlark, perched on a wooden fence, sang at Mullinville's round barn, which is on the National Register of Historic Places.

Along U.S. 400 at Mullinville, we photographed M.T. Liggett's political commentary. Pieces of his welded art act as kinetic sculptures, turned by the Kansas wind. Liggett is to scrap metal what Lucas' S.P. Dinsmoor was to concrete.

On either side of Greensburg, Mullinville and Haviland seemed like nurturing sisters, taking care of that tornado-battered town, offering services to its residents and the relief workers.

Dave and I could've easily spent a week touring the lefthand side of the state. Colorado is lovely of course, but if you head for a mountain vacation this summer, don't neglect western Kansas—where everything is in plain sight (even the hideouts.)

September 2007

ROUTE 66, ROUTE 7, 47, 59 . . .

When I left you last week, Dave and I were in Weir, Kansas, headed for Route 66.

We caught up with that most famous of highways in Galena. Galena is one of three towns in Kansas along Route 66. Of the 2,300 miles (give or take) of this historic roadway, only 13.2 miles ride through Kansas.

Galena (pop. 3,163) seems to be a town worn by hard times—and collapsing earth. The old mines below Galena are creating holes in the ground, which is causing big problems, as one might imagine.

You can find a couple of miles of the original Route 66 highway from Galena to the Missouri line. We drove the old narrow road to the state line and turned around.

Then, heading toward Oklahoma, we stopped at Eisler Brothers Store in Riverton (pop. 600). This business opened in 1925 and has a crowded-general-store feel to it. Cold drinks can be pulled from an old Coca-Cola chest, and a small room is packed with Route 66 souvenirs.

I asked the clerk about tourists, and she said it's quieter "now that the Norwegians are done for the season." She said groups from Norway rent motorcycles and ride from Chicago to Los Angeles or vice versa. International tourists stop in often.

"Many people come from England," she said. "And Spain. We get a lot from Spain."

Between Riverton and Baxter Springs stands the old Marsh Rainbow Arch bridge over Brush Creek. A new bridge has been built nearby, but the old span was preserved.

Route 66 winds through Baxter Springs (pop. 4,246) and into Oklahoma. The 13.2 miles were over in a hurry, but our journey was not complete; we took a different route home.

In Columbus (pop. 3,259), we found a beautiful fountain in front of the artsy Cherokee County Courthouse. A 1919 Seth Thomas clock tower, its workings visible inside a glass case, keeps time on the square.

On this trip, we tried to visit as many county seats as possible. The Crawford and Neosho county seats are not the largest towns in their counties. One might expect courthouses to be in Pittsburg and Chanute, but instead they are in Girard and Erie. First up, Girard (pop. 2,686).

On a corner of Girard's courthouse square is a memorial to veterans of the Vietnam War. There's a black, V-shaped wall with names of Kansans killed. Next to the wall is a helicopter from the war.

In Neosho County, Erie (pop. 1,167) has a low-flung modern courthouse. Across the street, there's a soda fountain in Richey's Rexall Drug Store.

On my many trips through southeast Kansas, I've seen the highway signs to Chanute, but have never entered the city limits. Until now.

Chanute (pop. 9,006) makes you glad you stopped. It's a pleasant place. The huge Santa Fe depot now houses the public library as well as the Osa and Martin Johnson Safari Museum. We'll have to return to explore that.

A cornerstone for Chanute is the Tioga Hotel, an impressive building in the heart of town.

Chanute is named for Octave Chanute, and downtown there's a creative, up-in-the-air memorial to the man who was a mentor to the Wright Brothers.

In Yates Center, Dave and I stopped for barbecue at Smokey Ben's. It's the place where I first enjoyed sweet potato fries a few years ago. Sweet potato fries should be on every restaurant menu and (to borrow *Gazette* columnist John Peterson's signature line), "they would be, if I had my way."

Route 66 is the road with the famed mystique. But in Kansas, every road, every highway unfolds with remnants of the old days. Each town in the state is worthy of exploration.

Follow your own route.

March 2010

LIVES OF ADVENTURE

I'm wondering how I've lived in the eastern half of the state for more than 25 years and have never visited the Martin and Osa Johnson Safari Museum in Chanute until now. A few weeks ago, Dave and I toured this impressive museum.

Martin Johnson was born in Illinois in 1884 and his family moved to Lincoln Center (Lincoln County), Kansas, a year later. When he was 11, they moved to Independence.

His father owned a jewelry store and had a Kodak franchise, selling cameras and photography supplies. Young Martin took it upon himself to learn everything he could.

Martin wrote to novelist Jack London and, at age 22, obtained a job as a cook on London's boat, the *Snark,* and sailed the South Seas for two years.

In 1909, Martin returned to Kansas. While regaling audiences with tales of his travels, he met 16-year-old Osa Leighty. Before long, Martin and Osa eloped to Kansas City. Previously, Osa had never been more than 35 miles from her home in Chanute. Six months after they married, the couple took Martin's *Snark* travelogue on the road, eventually performing on the Orpheum Vaudeville Circuit, earning money for an overseas trip.

They went off to the Solomon Islands, to Borneo and to Africa and photographed animals and natives, including headhunters and cannibals. The Martins were captured briefly by the Big Namba tribe, but a British patrol boat created an accidental diversion and the Johnsons made their escape.

Back in the United States, the Johnsons were a hit with their films. Besides being popular with audiences, their documentaries were helpful to the American Museum of Natural History, which helped the Johnsons secure funds for trips in the 1920s. George

Eastman, of Eastman Kodak, accompanied them on at least one African adventure.

Congorilla (1932) was the first movie with sound filmed entirely in Africa. Until then most people in the United States had never heard jungle sounds or the music of the African people.

Both Martin and Osa had pilot's licenses and purchased small planes, which enabled them to create aerial films. One of their planes was painted with zebra stripes, the other with giraffe spots.

Osa was reportedly handy with a Winchester rifle. When Martin did close-up photography on wild animals, it was Osa's job to cover him.

Martin said of his wife, "Osa had all the qualities that go to make an ideal traveling companion for an explorer—pluck, endurance and cheerfulness under discomfort."

The Johnsons spent 27 years together, documenting their adventures, making more than two dozen films and writing 18 books (including Osa's books for children). They survived the cannibals and the wild animals, but both died relatively young. Martin was killed at age 52 in a 1937 plane crash near Burbank, Calif., which also injured Osa. She died of a heart attack years later at age 58.

On the ground level of the Safari Museum (housed in Chanute's huge Santa Fe depot) is the Johnson Museum of African Culture, which is full of artifacts. You'll see dozens of masks, headdresses, some ancestor statues, drums and jewelry. The second floor of the museum is where the story of Martin and Osa Johnson is told in artifacts, words and photos.

The museum is a kid-friendly place with Young Explorer activities scattered around the museum. These include learning a few Swahili words, instructions for making an animal mask and instructions for making the board game Oware.

It's only 75 miles from Emporia to Chanute. Once there, the Safari Museum takes your mind on an adventure of its own. It's well worth the trip.

Safari Museum is at 111 N. Lincoln in Chanute. For more information, call 620-431-2730 or visit www.safarimuseum.com.

May 2009

MURPHY'S MERCANTILE

One question that invariably slides into my mind when I enter a Kansas town, especially a small one, is, "Is this a hospitable place?"

I guess on a deeper level the question really is, "Could I live here?" While I'm not likely to move anywhere anytime soon, it's always fun to try on a town to see how it feels around you.

Because I grew up in a community of about 400 people, I'm well aware of the small-town dramas and personality conflicts, but I also know the feeling of belonging and connectedness that comes from working side by side with neighbors and knowing the stories of their lives.

Recently, Dave and I pulled into a Neosho County town with about 105 souls—Stark.

We were returning to Emporia after spending several days in the Ozarks, and we had eaten lunch, Thai food at the Typhoon in Pittsburg. I was exhausted, reclining in the car's passenger seat. More than anything I just wanted to be home.

But Dave saw the road sign along K-39 and announced, "Stark. That sounds like a place we're obligated to check out."

I muttered a weak "OK," and he pulled into a field drive and turned the car around.

While Dave photographed the exterior of downtown buildings, I stepped into Murphy's Mercantile and Cafe. Two men were drinking coffee at the end of a long communal table. In a booth, a man and a woman were eating sandwiches.

I introduced myself to Denna Myers, who was working behind the counter. She told me a bit about this business, which Rick and Portia Murphy had owned for the past few years.

She bragged on the cook, Frances Stewart, listing some of

the favorite menu items and added, "She makes just a wonderful breakfast—with fresh hash browns."

A young man came in and ordered two sandwiches to go. He looked through the portal to the kitchen. "You've got Pete doing dishes?" he asked.

"We got busy for a Tuesday," Denna replied.

"Pete is the pastor of our church and he's helping out with dishes today," she told me. "He's a great guy."

The main room was the dining area, but a smaller room to the side held two aisles of groceries, cleaning supplies and garden seeds.

The place has a warm, country feel to it with wooden floors and tasteful décor. And even on that gloomy day with rain falling, the windows let natural light into Murphy's.

I could picture the large tables filling up in the morning with coffee drinkers. And they'd be laughing and teasing each other, because that's what people do who know each other well.

While photographing the restaurant, I glanced into a refrigerated case and spotted pie.

"Strawberry, chocolate and apple," Denna replied when I asked. She had made the pies herself from scratch.

You can probably guess: chocolate. I find it nearly impossible to resist the meringue-chocolate combination. I added a Diet Coke to the equation.

As I sat at the long table, which was scattered with auction bills, I pulled my birthday present from my pocket, an iPod Touch, and discovered: Wi-Fi! Yes, this place had wireless Internet.

A farmer, Lester Gemmill, came in for lunch and Dave and I visited with him about the incessant rain. Then Pete, the pastor, emerged from the kitchen and sat down with Lester.

Portia Murphy, the owner who was in Yates Center at a son's track meet, called while I was there. Denna handed me the phone and I met Portia via long distance. By now, I was beginning to feel like one of the family.

Twenty minutes at Murphy's and I felt revived. Caffeine, chocolate pie, cheerful conversation, and Wi-Fi—who needs more than that?

Seriously. Who needs more than that? I think I could live here.

September 2009

EXPLORERS VISIT HOWARD

Every hour on the hour, Howard residents can hear the ringing of the courthouse chimes.

It wasn't always so.

The Elk County Courthouse was built in 1908 with a clock tower. Funds ran short, so instead of inserting a real clock, four clock faces were painted on the building's tower. The time was right twice a day at 12:50. "It was always lunchtime," Shirley Black said of the fake clock.

Residents recently decided to get time moving in Howard; the community raised money. They put four glass clock faces in the tower with metal hands that actually move. The clock chimes on the hour and can play tunes including patriotic and Christmas melodies.

Shirley Black and other Howard residents spoke to more than 60 Kansas Explorers Club members on the courthouse lawn recently at a BYLOC (bring your own lawn chair) gathering in Howard.

These occasional BYOLC events showcase towns that have taken their destinies into their own hands, towns in which the residents work together to keep their communities energized.

Laura Fry, the Elk County Economic Development and Youth Coordinator, spoke of a new fitness center. The community bought 30 pieces of used commercial exercise equipment for only $1,000 from the town of Cherryvale. "And businesses in our community, without even being asked, came forward to pay the first six months' rent for the (fitness) building," Fry said.

Also, Fry mentioned that a $90,000 Heritage Trust Fund grant has been awarded so the county can put a new roof on the courthouse.

Pharmacist Julie Perkins told the Explorers that she's a hometown girl who left Howard in 1987 to attend the University of Kansas. At that time, she had no intention of ever returning to Howard to live. After college, she landed a job in Hutchinson. But after two years of working in the corporate world, Perkins jumped at the chance in 1995 to purchase the town's pharmacy (with soda fountain), Batson's Drug Store.

"It seemed natural to move back," she said. That move has allowed Perkins and her husband to raise their daughters in a small community.

Meanwhile, in 2004, the town's grocery store closed, which meant that residents would have to drive 30 minutes to Eureka or Sedan or 45 minutes to Winfield or Independence to purchase food.

Rather than let the town go without, the Perkinses decided to take on the grocery business. They added space, shifted the pharmacy around and put in a meat counter.

Perkins told the audience that on weekends she hauled her daughters "to the city" to buy groceries for the store. After two years of that time-consuming venture, she was thrilled to have a large enough food order so that groceries could be delivered to her.

"In 2006, we finally got our first grocery truck," she said.

They've recently purchased an adjacent building and will move the gift shop and soda fountain over to make more room for groceries.

Marci Penner of the Kansas Sampler Foundation added, "For Julie to even get the grocery truck to stop, she has to buy $7,500 worth of groceries a week."

And yes, that $7,500 is a weekly commitment. The town has about 750 people and she draws some customers from the outlying area. For her store to stay in business, area residents have to support the Family Market. And they do.

Explorers were told of other businesses and attractions: Poplar's Pizza, Toot's Drive-In, a soap maker, a downtown seamstress, a convenience store.

The American Legion is almost finished with the Veterans Memorial. Plans are developing for the renovation of the historic Howard National Bank building. Explorers were encouraged to investigate the city lake with its WPA structures as well as Hubbell's Rubble, Jerry Hubbell's colorful welded characters displayed along K-99.

Howard may appear to be a sleepy little town, but there's positive action afoot here. Residents can smile and remember that fact each time the courthouse clock chimes.

October 2009

WHAT A TOWN CREATES

When traveling the state, I like to look for something original in each town, something residents have created, restored or put on display. Unique projects help reflect a town's personality—they show how the locals have invested their time and money; you see what they value.

Argonia, in Sumner County, has built a half-mile walking and bike trail to the Chikaskia River. Shaded by trees with an occasional bench for resting, the sidewalk leads to a campground and picnic area, and then into the woods alongside the river.

In Harper County, Anthony residents have constructed a September 11 memorial with pieces of steel from the World Trade Center, honoring the heroic firefighters.

Up north in Waterville (Marshall County), the community spent years raising funds and restoring the 1905 Weaver Hotel, which reopened this year.

The Community Connection Trail gives walkers and bicyclists a safe path between Strong City and Cottonwood Falls. A restored foot bridge across the Cottonwood River is part of that trail. And Council Grove comes to mind with its gorgeous walkway along the Neosho River from downtown to the Kaw Mission Historic Site.

Last month, when Emporia Arts Council director Melissa Windsor announced that the building fund goal had been met, I happily added that to Emporia's list. The new arts center will be a dynamic resource for us all and something that visitors to town will envy.

In the 28 years I've lived in Emporia, time after time money has been raised for community projects that enhance our lives. I remember when a traveling exhibit of J. Seward Johnson

Jr. statues came to town in the late 1980s. Residents were so captivated with the bronze pieces that money was raised and one was purchased.

Just a Taste is the name of the statue chosen, featuring a boy, a girl and an ice cream cone. It stands in front of the Emporia Public Library. A plaque reads: "A gift to Emporia from the people of Emporia, December 1988."

If you want to see what Emporia can accomplish, just step inside the Granada Theatre. That's one big wow, especially if you remember it as the shabby Fox Theater in the 1980s or if you saw it during its gutted restoration phase. Now, the Granada is Emporia's shining star, thanks to folks like John Mallon, who had long-range vision and put heart and money into the massive undertaking. This was a community-supported project; we all made it happen.

Community donations also made possible the *Spring in the Flint Hills* mural on the side of the Java Cat-5 building near Sixth and Merchant. During the spring of 2003, Louis Copt and Stan Herd climbed a scaffold and painted that picture for us.

The project of one Leadership Emporia class was the *Our Flag Was Still There* mural at Eleventh and Commercial. Emporia has also created an impressive Veterans Memorial Park and holds a celebration every November in honor of veterans.

The playground at Peter Pan Park was initiated by another Leadership Emporia class. Hundreds of volunteers built that playground during a week in May 2008.

For years, the Emporia Eastside Community Group plotted and planned, along with the city, the development of the Eastside Memorial Park at Ninth and East Streets. In 2006, the park had a solitary swingset. That was it. Now there's a magnificent new playground area with several swingsets, and up the hill is a large shelter house. The newest addition to the park is an obelisk sculpted by Alan Tollakson and Fletcher Russell.

These projects are joint efforts. We rely on each other, the city and county, businesses, schools, the university, churches, and service organizations, because it's by working together that we accomplish great things.

These are just some of the gifts we've given ourselves, things that improve our quality of life and make Emporia unique.

Now with the construction of the new arts center under way, we can watch another project in progress in the 800 block of Commercial.

Visitors to town should be impressed. Heck, we should be impressed. Emporians can take pride in what our generation has created.

May 2004

DEMENTIA CONCRETIA

Get me a bag of cement; I want to make some art.

On a recent Saturday, my friend Karla and I toured several small towns near her Lincoln County residence.

The art scene in Lucas is a trip into eccentric minds—but it's a fun trip. My theory is that Lucas sits on some sort of vortex where weird, yet creative energies swirl. Something compels a number of residents of north central Kansas to make grassroots art, also known as intuitive, outsider, or visionary art.

Many of you are familiar with the Garden of Eden in Lucas, the bizarre creation of Samuel P. Dinsmoor (1843–1932). When he was 64, Dinsmoor began his elaborate project. He built a limestone home in the style of a log cabin. Over the next 22 years, he used 113 tons of cement to construct trees and figures in his very own Biblical/political theme park.

This was a man with a passion.

On the Roadside America Website, I found an explanation of the creative obsession of some retirees: "A strange earwig burrows into their brain and forces them to build, Build, BUILD! Taking whatever is handy—usually concrete, bottles and household junk—they fashion icons and structures until they are exhausted. This is dementia concretia. Whatever its cause, it prolongs the lives of the afflicted."

Karla and I took a guided tour of the Grassroots Arts Center in downtown Lucas. Adult admission was $5.50, and well worth it. Inside the arts center was the work of another man drawn to cement. On his farm south of Lucas, Ed Root made hundreds of sculptures from concrete, broken glass and stone. The bright blue pieces of glass came from Milk of Magnesia bottles, the green from 7Up bottles. "After his wife died, he broke up her dishes and used them in his work," our tour guide said.

But there's more to grassroots art than concrete.

One of my favorite pieces was a sculpture made from found objects. When a lake in MacArthur Park in Los Angeles was drained, one man picked out the junk that had been tossed into the water. He designed a complex piece using a couple of hundred small items: marbles, dice, jewelry, false teeth, a handgun.

And Herman Divers of Topeka built a two-seater car constructed of those aluminum pull-tabs from pop and beer cans. He also made garments, furniture, and a motorcycle from pull-tabs.

From the Grassroots Arts Center, Karla and I were directed a few blocks away to the Florence Deeble home.

Deeble's creative impulse took hold in the '50s when her mother, fearful of a child drowning in their small fish pond, asked her to fill in the pond with concrete. Deeble lived near Dinsmoor's Garden of Eden and his work made an impression on her. Much of the Deebles' backyard is covered with painted concrete landscapes: Mount Rushmore and Lucas Lake, mountain and desert scenes. She died in 1999 at age 99.

There are younger grassroots artists as well. Jim Dickerman, of Beverly, makes things out of animal bones and car and machine parts. Besides what is shown in the arts center, Dickerman displays his sculptures in roadside pastures along Kansas Highway 18. Some of his works of art turn in the wind.

Before the trip, I had asked Karla for directions to her house in Beverly. She instructed me to take a left at the dragon. "Yes, a dragon," she wrote. Dickerman's wildly painted "Dream Dragon" was built from farm equipment and is about 20 feet tall.

Maybe there is a creative vortex at Lucas. At the arts center I felt a rush of energy—a strong urge to produce something myself. Karla also enjoyed seeing the artwork.

"I really do kind of like this stuff—and that scares me," Karla said with a smile.

July 2009

THE RED HILLS

The Red Hills in south-central Kansas may be the most color-rich region of the state.

Running between the county seats of Barber and Comanche counties is the Gypsum Hills Scenic Byway, one of the state's nine scenic byways.

This byway through the Red/Gypsum Hills is 42 miles long, from Medicine Lodge to Coldwater. There are a couple of turnouts where you can stop to view the hills, but if you really want to learn the land you can leave the highway and wander off on some of the red dirt roads in Barber County.

Turning onto a side road immerses you in the landscape. As you step out of your car, a deep breath fills you with the welcoming fragrance of Kansas—the weedy smell of summertime.

Dark greens and sage greens contrast with the deep red earth. White gypsum streaks the red mesas and buttes. Add a blue sky for background, some passing clouds and well, it's just hard to beat this place if you're looking for simple and natural beauty.

The solitude here reminds me of Chase County's back roads. In the Gypsum Hills you may hear singing insects and chirping birds, and you may spot a band of curious deer. The mesas, the cedars and the red sand roads begin to take you over. You may not want to leave.

A trip to the Red Hills is a journey of three to four hours from Emporia. Dave and I took off early one Friday evening, jumped on the Kansas Turnpike and trusted that there would be a motel in Medicine Lodge.

After passing through Wichita, we encountered small communities I'd never heard of: Schulte, Clonmel, Suppesville.

Kansas continues to surprise me—there's always something "new" to discover.

At dusk, we passed through Harper, a town with a red fish atop the water tower and a 1909 fountain in the middle of Main Street.

We did find a motel in Medicine Lodge. And, as we left it about 7:30 the next morning, Dave said, "If we were *National Geographic* photographers, we'd have been in the field two hours ago."

Alas, we are not with *National Geographic,* but rather just two people who needed sleep and a shower. To use what was left of the angled morning light, however, Dave and I skipped breakfast and headed for the hills.

We photographed the rugged red terrain south of U.S. 160. As the sun climbed in the sky, clouds moved in, eclipsing the morning rays. So we headed west down the highway.

A welcome sign read: "Coldwater—the way life should be."

There's a hospital here in this town of 774, and a swimming pool. Dave said, "Coldwater Swimming Pool—that doesn't sound too inviting."

"What's the best thing about Coldwater?" I asked our waitress when we stopped for a late breakfast at the Timberwolf Café.

"It's quiet," she said. "And everybody knows everybody. If you need help, you can ask. It's not like in a big city where people say 'I don't have time to help.'"

There is a warm hometown feel in Coldwater. As Dave and I walked around on a Saturday morning, folks waved as they drove past and people on the sidewalks easily engaged in conversations with us.

As I contemplated the possibilities that could be inside a storefront called the Coldwater Pleasure Club, a man stepped out of the post office nearby, so I asked him, "Hey, what's in the Pleasure Club?"

"Oh, that's a place where men play dominoes and pool and cards," he said. "Yeah, I grew up in Protection (15 miles away) and when we came to Coldwater when I was a kid, I wondered the same thing. But that's what it is."

Coldwater has the Chief, a restored 1928 theater. There's

the Comanche County Courthouse with pots of petunias and geraniums at the front door, and Heritage Park, which honors those who died for our country during wartime and peacetime.

After Dave and I walked through a partially renovated hotel, petted a sweet young cat and photographed the grain elevators, it was time to head east and see what else we could find in south-central Kansas.

Earth and Sky

February 2003

A TALE OF TWO LANDSCAPES

Today I bought a card to send to my favorite uncle. He celebrates a birthday next week.

Uncle Jay is married to my mom's sister, Norma. Jay is my topographical sparring partner. We have a landscape rivalry, similar to arguing over who has the better football team. It's a good-natured volley between the Kansan and the Arkansan.

Jay pokes fun at the flat land of Kansas and I tease him about the clutter of trees and the interference of hills in the Arkansas scenery. Aunt Norma, a one-time Kansas resident, referees (well, sometimes she instigates the dissention).

A while back, Norma gave my mother an oil painting that Norma had painted years before. In the painting, an old, converted round-top school bus rests near a tree. The remainder of the landscape is minimal: an electrical pole and line, the horizon, grass, sky.

"Actually, Jay wanted me to get rid of the painting," Norma said. "He thought it was too depressing. He thought it looked like. . . ." She stopped and turned toward me. "Well, I don't want to say around you."

But she grinned and continued. "Well, he thought it looked like Kansas."

Jay explained in his Arkansas drawl, "It looks like people went out to pick wheat, their bus broke down and they've lost all hope."

Yeah, we Kansans expect these jabs. That's just part of our birthright.

Jay grew up in Arkansas and he practiced medicine in southern Missouri. Now he's back in his home state along with Norma and my mother, all of whom are native Arkansans.

Seldom has Jay wandered across the Kansas border. For a short time their daughter, Cindy, lived in Hutchinson. Jay and Norma flew to visit her soon after Jay earned his pilot's license. Finally, he acknowledged one benefit to the flatness of Kansas: "The whole darned state is a landing field!"

What Jay dislikes about Kansas is exactly what I love—the openness. In the Arkansas hills, I feel confined. What I see are walls of trees. Ahead, trees. Around the curve, trees. Even at the top of a hill, there's no view, just more trees.

Now tell me, how do people who live in the hills make it through the day without a horizon? Aren't they curious about sunrises and sunsets? And just how do they measure time when they can't follow a cloud all the way across the sky?

While visiting with my uncle one day, I described the book about Kansas that I've started and how many more pages I needed to complete it. In a typical Jay response, he said, "If you want it to really be like Kansas, you can just put in a lot of blank pages."

How could I not love this guy?

Jay and I merely judge landscape on two different scales. While I find the Arkansas hills to be claustrophobic and intimidating, to Jay they are comforting; they are home. Maybe we don't have a choice. Perhaps the environment into which we are born is as unshakable as our genes.

February 2003

PEOPLE OF THE SOUTH WIND

I've finally figured out what constitutes a "nice" weather day in Kansas. It doesn't matter whether it's cloudy or clear, warm or cold; a nice day is a day without wind.

A few weeks ago, on those January mornings when temperatures of 4 and 7 degrees ran up our heating bills, I heard several people say, "It's not that bad outside—the wind's not blowing."

Ten miles per hour is a slow wind day for us. However, in the winter, even a light breeze invokes the windchill factor and can make it feel like –13 or –48 degrees, a cold you can't imagine until it slaps bare skin.

Denim is better than nothing, of course, but even heavy jeans won't save you from a bitter Kansas gale. And gusts here seldom compare with the western half of the state. They never have plain old snow in western Kansas. Instead, they experience blowing and drifting snow.

Kansa is a Sioux word with "people of the south wind" as its common and suitable interpretation. Wind in Kansas—few things in life are as certain.

Maybe it's part of the midwestern work ethic that makes air discontent to laze around in Kansas. Wind is always on the move, seeking a balance, chasing itself from high to low pressure. We deal with it the best we can—we unconsciously lower our center of gravity, lean our heads into the blast and let it recklessly part our hair.

When I asked a newcomer her opinion of the Kansas landscape, a woman from Washington state replied, "Well, I don't like the wind." Wind as landscape, that's accurate. It may be fleeting but it is as permanent as the topography.

Wind always has sound, but sometimes that becomes obvious only when there is absolutely no breeze at all. An eeriness rises. Dead silence. The world has stopped breathing.

Like eyes adjusting to the dark, ears must adapt to the quiet. Soon I'm able to discern the crisp words of a conversation half a block away and hear rustling as the cat creeps through the grass. Every sound is enunciated, defined, heard as if for the first time.

When I first put on glasses at age 9, I discovered that trees and buildings were outlined in black. Objects had edges. I'd had no idea. And it's like that with sound, too. Without wind, sound has edges. Each sound begins and ends.

Some might believe that the noise of wind is the clamor of a windmill churning helplessly, or the snapping of sheets on the clothesline. But on the prairie, with no trees to whip around, no panes of glass to rattle, there is an omnipresent roar, somewhat oceanic, as transient air flees unhindered for the border. In town, the fugitive wind leaves behind the appearance of a crime scene: ransacked yards, potted plants knocked over, trash cans rolling down the street.

My mother, who often complained about our rambunctious wind, bragged when she moved from Kansas to Georgia, "I can leave a newspaper on the picnic table in the morning and in the evening it's still open to the same page."

Now, even on a tranquil day in Kansas, that newspaper would be stuck in a Nebraska fence by nightfall.

In a discussion group, a man said, "After living in Seattle for a few years, I came back to Kansas and when I felt the wind that's when I knew I was home."

In the months ahead, the wind will slug us from the south, bending trees during their growing season, curving them into question marks. A sunny 73-degree day will beg you to take a walk, a pleasant interlude, but 35 mph gusts will jump at you like a Labrador puppy. The strong breeze blows dust into your eyes, rearranges your clothes and rubs the fine hair on your arms the wrong way.

In Kansas, we learn early on that there is no hair spray strong enough for the battle. Wind is part of the landscape here. It's how I know I am home.

January 2007

ON THE HORIZON

With the anniversary of statehood coming up on Monday, it's time once again to reflect on what makes Kansas, Kansas.

And what Kansas is, is flat.

Oh, don't yell at me, I know Kansas isn't absolutely flat; there are bumps on that grassy skin of ours. We have rolling hills, but still, you have to admit there is a pleasing smoothness to the state.

The stark landscape alarms visitors, but we Kansans are pleased to gaze toward the west and see nothing but that steady line in the distance. And on occasion we find ourselves thinking that the setting sun is like the centered bubble on a carpenter's level.

In Kansas we can look in any direction and find that balanced line. In fact, the horizon forms a big hoop—this straight line encircles us. The flatness of landscape lets our eyes aim for distance. When we're out on the plains, we can see 5, 10, maybe 15 miles ahead.

While driving during daylight, we see the contours of the earth, the soft hills, the valleys. At twilight, the rounded shapes flatten and the view becomes an abstract painting: a heavy slab of straight earth, a swath of darkening sky and that horizontal line between them.

I love the Kansas horizon—the simple, clean line that defines the heavens and the earth. It's a narrow line, as thin as a guitar string.

Now you'd think, wouldn't you, that the horizon would be a bold, thick, Magic Marker of a line, one that, in effect, says, "Warning: The earth stops here! Take one more step and you're a goner!"

And perhaps, posted at the end of the earth, there is a sign announcing that danger.

None of us have been to the edge. I've driven fast, I've driven far, but I've never reached that narrow line. But if I ever did stumble upon the horizon, I would lie flat on my stomach, my face hanging over the edge of buffalo grass, and I'd peek into the blackness where stars are used as stepping stones.

Kansas is flat; the earth is round—a contradiction of shapes.

Now, we've known about the Niña, the Pinta and the Santa Maria ever since second grade; our minds have always had to reconcile the level land with a round planet. It may be a sphere, but the earth does have edges — beyond which the sun appears and disappears.

The sun rises like a waking cat, sleepy eyed, unhurried. With a show of creamy blues, Easter pinks and blinding yellows, the sun finally stretches its long light across the eastern sky.

But in the evening, the Kansas sun does not go quietly into that dark night. It crosses the finish line in a fiery battle, shooting flares as if it's going down for the very last time.

It flings color into the sky and onto the clouds — a kaleidoscope of lavender, scarlet, and tangerine. You train your eyes for subtle changes, afraid to glance away lest you miss the coral-to-crimson moment. And then before you're ready to let go, the colors fade, the sky empties. Darkness falls. And we sleep in the shadow of the earth.

We are the lucky ones, for every day our eyes rest naturally upon that horizon, that thin line of magic that holds together the heavens and the earth.

June 2003

VANISHING POINTS

The other day as I drove toward Olpe, it occurred to me that here in eastern Kansas, we're a little short on vanishing points. Highways and dirt roads disappear behind a hill or a slight rise, sometimes a curve, before they have any chance of vanishing in the distance.

The landscape of western Kansas, however, is a different story: flat and flatter.

When I was 8, Ruth Deckert, my Sunday school teacher, taught me and my 10-year-old brother art lessons at her farmhouse kitchen table. Ruth explained the concept to us.

"When two parallel lines, one on either side of you, meet at the horizon, that is called a vanishing point," she said.

With a sketch, Ruth showed us that these parallel lines—ditches, the edges of a road, fences on either side—do converge way off in the distance.

My question was: If I sent my obnoxious brother down that road, would he, too, vanish?

After that art lesson, I noticed, as I looked down certain mile roads in Barton County, that the fence posts on either side of the road did aim toward a point, far away, one dot in the center of the picture.

This concept works on flat land, and western Kansas is an ideal place to look toward the horizon and watch roads disappear, left and right.

Although the High Plains and all of the state is on a gradual slope, rising in altitude to meet the Rocky Mountains, much of the land in the southwest part of the state is checkerboard flat. It's as if the ceaseless wind blew away the rises and falls of the earth and the summer sun ironed out the remaining wrinkles.

Western Kansas is all about distance: distance between

towns, between farms, between people. Some counties near the Colorado border average three people per square mile.

Out there, solitude is a survival skill. Rural residents know that there may be days between conversations, and that forgetting something at the grocery store 30 miles away means doing without.

Birds fly for miles between branches and light on one scrappy hedge tree under which a handful of cattle huddle in its shade.

On this endless plane, small towns are marked by grain elevators, which crop up like white pins stuck in the rectangular map. These rural monuments can be seen for miles. Elevators give the traveler something to focus on, a target, a town (and perhaps a public restroom—few and far between in these parts).

Sometimes on the lonesome Kansas Highway 156 from Larned to Garden City, you might gallop along for half an hour without seeing another car. With the luxury of no hills and no curves, it's kind of disappointing that there are also no vehicles to pass.

On this level land, it feels as if you are standing in a snow globe. The blue sky is an overhead dome and the line of horizon forms a complete circle, with you at the center. Columbus was right, the earth is round.

In this vacant space, peripheral vision is ensured. Without turning our heads, we can see beside ourselves, behind us. Everything is in plain sight. If you look down any mile road, you'll see that it aims toward a tiny point in the distance. The roadway appears to vanish. All around you, fields stretch to the horizon, where even the planet fades away, curving into itself.

And that brother of mine, no longer obnoxious, did disappear one day from these Kansas roads. He drove north, then west, and made his home in Alaska.

It's odd, out on the flat land where there is nowhere to hide, that this is the place where people and things vanish right before our eyes.

June 2005

NO PLACE TO FALL

At least 20 homes were destroyed as residences tumbled down a hill during a recent landslide in Laguna Beach, Calif. After a winter of heavy rains, land gave way early one morning and a neighborhood self-destructed. Residents wearing bedclothes ran for their lives as they heard and felt their homes breaking apart. More often than one would expect, houses crash down California mountainsides.

That's one thing about Kansas. For the most part, our land stays put. It doesn't wander hither and yon, reshaping the scenery at will. Not so you'd notice anyway. Kansas has a sinkhole or two, but no violent landslides. Earthquakes are possible and have occurred in this region, but I've never felt one.

And, of course, in Kansas, should the earth ever decide to wiggle or fidget, we have nowhere to fall to. When your land starts out as an ocean floor, well, that just seems like an unlikely place to drop from.

The earth, the landscape, in both California and Kansas, is always changing and eroding, in some places faster than others. Time, weather and gravity take their toll and mountains crumble. Some states spend a lot of money on "Watch for Falling Rocks" signs. Not Kansas.

The only things that fall on us are rain, hail, snow and funnel clouds. If you scroll down the menu of natural disasters in Kansas, you'll find droughts, floods, tornadoes and grasshopper plagues, but there's no listing for falling boulders or buildings.

Kansas has no mountains, but that doesn't mean we're deprived. This far-reaching land provides serenity. It's a low-key place with an understated beauty.

In an essay called "A Level Land," William Inge, an

Independence native, wrote, "No mountains can be as beautiful for me as the far horizon, level as a floor, 20 or 30 miles in the distance. The sight so fills me with a wonderful feeling of personal freedom, and also with a sense of infinity."

The simple landscape here is something I've always appreciated. But then, I'm a minimalist and the prairie is Zen-like with its simple and clean lines. This is the state that made two-dimensional land famous—you know, with that whole "flatter than a pancake" reputation.

Our third dimension comes primarily from structures. In the nearly treeless western Kansas, there's not much that's vertical out there except for man-made objects such as grain elevators and radio towers.

In his book *Wolf Willow,* Wallace Stegner discusses the Canadian plains, but his words about the horizontal landscape are just as valid for western Kansas:

". . . the world is flat, empty, nearly abstract, and in its flatness you are a challenging upright thing, as sudden as an exclamation mark, as enigmatic as a question mark."

Isn't that a great line?

And Stegner suggests that level land is the earth's destiny.

"Nature abhors an elevation as much as it abhors a vacuum; a hill is no sooner elevated than the forces of erosion begin tearing it down.

"These prairies are quiescent, close to static; looked at for any length of time, they begin to impose their awful perfection on the observer's mind. Eternity is a peneplain."

So the surface of the earth intends, desires to be flat. It's one of the planet's long-range goals. Which means, naturally, that the rest of the world is trying to catch up with us.

As William Allen White once said (albeit in a different context), "When anything is going to happen in this country, it happens first in Kansas."

Before long, others will recognize Kansas as the "it" state, the leader of the pack.

Which is a status we've assumed all along.

January 2006

ANOTHER DAY IN PARADISE

I've never lived in another state.

My entire life, the gregarious sky over Kansas has been my constant companion.

I've seen our clouds drop tornadoes and I've been pelted by sleet and hail. Leaks in these skies have drenched me. The sun's rays have soaked into the pores of my skin and each April the sun's warmth erases any memory of winter. Kansas winds have blown mosquitoes off my arms and its gusts have tangled my fine hair into knots.

Below my feet, the long-reaching prairies have kept me grounded.

In the Flint Hills, I've leapt from stone to stone without splashing into the grass that ripples across the land. Out here the buckskin-colored pastures are anchored by fence posts, push pins, which keep the turf from rolling up and blowing away with a gale-force breeze.

You could remove me from these fruited plains, relocate me in another part of the country, and I'd probably still thrive, but I'd sure as heck miss Kansas.

Sometimes when a person becomes overly familiar with a region, the scenery disappears and one's fascination of the place diminishes. With Kansas though, I can't seem to get enough. I want to take it all in—investigate each angle of history, learn the names of birds and wildflowers, face the west for every carnival-colored sunset.

Kansas offers the unusual: a rattlesnake roundup, an outhouse tour, the Garden of Eden. This place has also given us jackrabbits, ring-necked pheasants and plesiosaurs (though not necessarily in that order). Our history includes American

Indians, explorers and immigrants, railroaders, soldiers and aviators. We can study cattle drives and politics, the Santa Fe Trail and Bleeding Kansas.

In the tiny town of Wabaunsee, you'll find the Beecher Bible and Rifle Church. Victoria is proud of its Cathedral of the Plains. At Heartland Farm near Pawnee Rock, their chapel is a converted silo.

Kansas covers nearly 83,000 square miles, but there's no way to measure its magnificence and beauty. On this landlocked prairie, we have an expanse the size of a sea. We stand on the floor of that long-gone ocean which once reflected starry nights and we hear phantom waves that roar like the wind. When the earth rose and the sea drained, we were left with shark teeth in the dirt and fossils embedded in tomes of limestone—their stories we read again and again.

The openness of Kansas gives us space to balance our accounts. When alone on these pastures, worries vanish from our hearts just as easily as clouds float across county lines.

Secrets and mysterious buildings linger in small towns. The air in Williamsburg fills with a thick aroma of smoked ribs coming from Guy and Mae's Tavern, a Kansas landmark. In Homewood, which is something of a ghost town, a black and white cat slips under a sheet metal fence and disappears. On a cool morning in Princeton, a young couple returns from a bicycle ride on the Prairie Spirit Trail.

Meanwhile, above the fields in Franklin County, a bald eagle soars. A dozen or so cow-calf pairs stand close in a pasture and winter wheat is a bright patch of green that shocks the monochrome landscape. Parked in the shadow of a swayback barn, a grandfather's tractor waits for the farmer to return.

We are lucky to live in this state, which offers endless skies, mood-altering sunsets, and enough space for us to understand the meaning of freedom.

Our forefathers drew a rectangle around paradise and called it Kansas.

We call it home.

Happy Kansas Day.

March 2006

THE DRAMA QUEEN

The Kansas sky is such a drama queen. She'll do anything for attention. One day, she's a sleek debutante, showing off a sapphire-colored silk gown. The next day she's a crazed, wild-haired woman chasing us with a band of psychotic clouds.

Queenie is all over the behavioral spectrum, especially during these springtime months. We observe our matriarch in her dressing room, changing from solid blue to frilly lace to dowdy gray. Sometimes her outfits are bridal white; half the time they're as black as night.

She wields incredible power. The queen rescues us from winter with a sun so warm that it tickles our skin. Her spring rains color the grass green again, and she flirts with flowers to make them bloom.

When she's depressed, Her Royal Highness casts a pall over the land. She wraps the sun in a ratty chenille bathrobe and smothers our light.

And on her angriest days, the queen is a killing machine. In her fury, she thunders and stomps and reaches down to earth with electrical claws. Her palms sweep the ground, leaving wreckage and twisted trees.

But when she's at the top of these mood swings, it's her sparkling hours that make 7-year-old girls skip on the sidewalk.

On cheerful days, the entire neighborhood turns out to play. Dogs tug at their leashes. Joggers seem to hang in mid-air stride. Car windows are open and music dances down the street.

While the Kansas landscape is serene and immobile, the air is alive with color and animation. Above us is where the action lies: the sky is the prize.

Seventy-degree days draw me out onto the front porch. My

feet push against the railing as I balance on the back legs of a metal chair. I'll pretend to read a book, but I'm really out there to watch the clouds.

On clear afternoons, I find myself staring as far into outer space as my eyes will take me. I try to reach the back end of that box of blue. I know there must be black on the other side, but I can't quite see that far.

With no landmarks in the sky, it's impossible to know how far we can see. Are those clouds to the east casting shadows on Lebo? Or Beto Junction? Only when the blue air is freckled with cumulus, can we even begin to guess the size of the sky. But how many clouds can fit over the ground space that is Lyon County? And how big is a cloud? Is it the size of a city block or as large as square mile?

There's always something going on up there. The map of the sky continually redraws itself.

Cross-country jets leave razor-thin trails which bloat, then dissolve. Cumulus follow each other across the sky like words on a page. Lonely, uncertain clouds are lost in the whim of wind.

Before our eyes, the sky transforms, becomes a new character. Thunderheads build and darkness overtakes the day. The tempest whips us with rain and hail.

"Look at me! Look at me!" the drama queen shouts.

And we can't help but look. Each morning, a new sky jumps out to surprise us; we live our lives between danger and delight.

Spring is both tranquil and turbulent. But no matter what happens, we always return to a clear sky, a clean slate.

December 2003

A THIN PLACE

Standing on the stone arch bridge at Clements, I hear only silence.

Gradually, the background noise shifts into the present moment. A few birds chatter. A dog barks in the distance. Water gurgles as it slips downstream in the Cottonwood River.

Earlier on that warm Sunday in November, my husband and I enjoyed breakfast alongside the motorcyclists at the Emma Chase Café in Cottonwood Falls. The biker breakfast was quite a meal: a biscuit with gravy, bacon, link sausage, scrambled eggs, hash browns and another biscuit for the homemade apple butter.

Full and happy, Dave and I then drove west on U.S. 50, past Elmdale and the Clover Cliff Ranch.

We turned at Clements, a tiny town past its prime, to visit the stone arch bridge, which is on the National Register of Historic Places. Built in 1886 by the L.P. Santy Co., the bridge has two high and graceful arches and is made of large rectangular chunks of native limestone.

I leaned my forearms on that stone bridge and glanced up at a swath of cirrus clouds in the thin blue sky. The sun was warm, the air still. It felt like home.

Trips into the Flint Hills always restore me to a sense of wholeness. I feel those lost parts of myself return.

I imagine that most people know of a place where they feel renewed and complete. One person might feel most at home while hiking a mountain trail, another at a farm pond with a fishing line in the water.

Sometimes I drive through the open range east of Matfield Green. My car rattles over the cattle guards; it fords rock-bottomed streams.

In many places on the open range, other than your vehicle and the road it is on, there is nothing man-made in sight: no fences, no houses, no power poles. You'll see only grassy hills dotted with white rocks, scattered as if flung from above.

These gravel roads wind like rivers, pulling me up and around the hills. At the edge of the roadway, grass flows ever outward, spreading like a chain reaction.

Now, chlorophyll has slithered back into the ground. The November fields reflect various shades of umber, sienna, ocher. Tops of little bluestem catch the sun and look like magical wands, white and luminescent.

I am drawn to the open landscape, the uncluttered space. A sense of freedom comes with this unobstructed view.

These hills haven't changed much in 10,000 years, I'm told. Before this region became a rocky pasture, it was an inland sea—about 300 million years ago during the Permian Period of the Paleozoic Era.

Here on the lonely prairie, I begin to understand the irrelevance of time, the reach of infinity.

This is a sacred landscape.

On a Sunday morning last winter, I drove south on the Kansas Turnpike to visit a friend in Wichita. I left Emporia before sunrise. Few cars were out on the highway. I had the road, the sky and the scenery all to myself.

Just outside Emporia, the turnpike tumbles into the Flint Hills. The earth flows like huge ocean waves, brown undulations, rising and falling.

While I drove, light pulled itself into the eastern sky.

Form is everything. Sky is everything. Light is everything.

That morning, as the sun tipped above the horizon, it charged the highest rises of earth with vigorous beams. The land had only two colors: shadow and light.

In *Living Between Worlds,* Philip Sheldrake mentions "'a thin place' where the membrane between this world and the other world, between the material and the spiritual, was very permeable."

There are moments, if one is lucky enough, to be in both worlds at once.

January 2008

IN BETWEEN

Eastbound on Highway 56 in central Kansas, I glance into my side mirror and see the buttery sun, liquid at the horizon, vanish for the day. It's a December evening. I am traveling alone, headed home to Emporia. I am between places, between here and there.

Around me, the sky clings to blue for a while, but its grasp loosens and the light runs away with the sun. As daylight escapes behind me, I drive toward the dark end of the road.

When the sun leaves this plane of earth, color goes with it. Darkness lands, turning the world to a grainy charcoal, then black, and my range of vision closes in on every side.

Overhead, the three-quarters moon keeps watch on the roadway, that moon surrounded by a posse of stars.

I drive my car into the world of deep mysteries, where nothing seems to exist outside the reach of headlight beams, where trees dissolve into the landscape, where the topography on either side levels out into one thin line.

I turn off the radio and hear, feel, the hum of road noise. Winter pulls the drone of the tires into the cab of the car. Every sound echoes in the cold, in the dark.

Highway noise at night brings back childhood memories of curling up in the backseat of the family car. But that lullaby of tires can also put a driver to sleep—and that's not a place a driver should go.

In this tunnel of night, when another car approaches, its headlights capture my eyes and I fight being drawn into a trance.

My car and I have slipped into that other world . . . that in-between world . . . in between departure and arrival, the world of being in movement, of not belonging to a particular place or time.

As I drive through the night, I imagine myself sailing through outer space. In the distance, galaxies of stars turn out to be small towns: Galva, Canton, Hillsboro, Marion. I pass under each cluster of streetlights briefly before entering another canyon of black space.

Darkness swallows barns and tractors, round hay bales and distant shelterbelts. When you cannot see the farmhouses, or the driveways, or the power poles that you're passing, there's no sense of making any progress. White stripes in the center of the road repeat themselves like a treadmill belt. Other vehicles on the highway are anonymous, their colors indistinguishable, the occupants unseen.

Out in the vast wilderness of night, there's a feeling of separateness. I'm cocooned in the cabin of the car, cold leaking in through the glass, headlights shining on the road, blackness everywhere else.

While hurtling through the void, I am between places, in limbo. I am between the past and the future. I am untethered, free-floating.

Sometimes it feels good to be ungrounded, unrestricted, wandering in the world of all possibilities.

Under the moon and the starry, starry sky, all I have to do is keep the car between the center line and the shoulder and let the highway pull me home.

ABOUT THE AUTHOR

Cheryl Unruh began writing her weekly Flyover People column for The Emporia Gazette in 2003. Her writing has received awards from the Kansas Press Association, the Kansas Association of Broadcasters and the Kansas Sampler Foundation. Cheryl's commentaries have aired on Kansas Public Radio in Lawrence, and KTWU, public television in Topeka.

Cheryl was raised in the small town of Pawnee Rock in central Kansas and graduated from the University of Kansas in Lawrence. She lives in Emporia, Kansas, with her husband, Dave Leiker.

More of Cheryl's columns and daily writings may be read at www.flyoverpeople.net.

Dave's Kansas photos can be seen at www.flyoverpeople.net/galleries.htm.